FIGHT BACK & WIN

Bottom Line/Publishing publishes the advice of expert authorities in many fields. The use of this material is not a substitute for legal, accounting, health or other professional services. Consult a competent professional for answers to your specific questions.

Library of Congress Cataloging-in-Publication Data
Fight Back and Win
p.cm.
ISBN 0-88723-172-1

Bottom Line/Publishing is an imprint of Boardroom® Inc.
55 Railroad Ave., Greenwich, CT 06830

Printed in the United States of America
Distributed by Capital Books

Acknowledgements

I am sincerely grateful to a host of people who made this book possible. I shall always remember how especially fortunate I am to have so many wonderful and dedicated colleagues who helped make this book a reality.

First and foremost I would like to thank **Martin Edelston** and all of his hardworking staff, in particular **Nancy Crowfoot**, at Boardroom Inc. They made this book possible by assisting and encouraging me to bring valuable information about HMOs and health insurance to the public at a time when these issues have become one of the critical national issues of the day. I shall always be indebted to them for the confidence they have given me by allowing me to be the author for this book as well as an author for their magnificent "Bottom Line" subscription publications.

To **Kathleen Hughes** and all of the marvelous people at Capital Books, for their excellent design of the cover and for their willingness to distribute this book to the public. Their superb advice and guidance was most helpful and appreciated.

To **Rick Frishman** and all the people at Planned Television Arts, and in particular **Sandy Trupp** and **Maureen Chase**, who helped coordinate everything from the beginning. There are no better people around when it comes to getting a book out there for public consumption.

To my assistant on this project, **Carla Levenson**, for working by my side and coordinating, editing, writing, and doing everything necessary to make this book a reality. Her contribution for putting this book together was priceless and I cannot thank her enough for her valuable assistance from beginning to end.

To **Marion Buhagiar**, our editor, who made this book better by her insightful editing and sharing with us the depth of her experience.

To **Jamie Court** of Consumers for Quality Care, for his dogged work on behalf of consumers and for contributing the "Casualty of the Day" case histories in this book. CQC is the HMO patients' watchdog thanks to Jamie's tireless efforts at exposing HMO abuses.

To my friend and law partner extraordinaire, **Mike Bidart,** who pioneered the HMO litigation in our law firm and has been responsible for forcing many reforms in HMO practices by his successful court cases. He is the most loyal, dedicated, and hardworking lawyer I have ever met and I am indeed fortunate to enjoy his support and faith.

To my wonderful law partner **Frank Darras,** who wrote the chapters in this book on disability and has become a national expert on disability insurance. Frank spearheads our law firm's health insurance department and works tirelessly on behalf of consumers. I will always be appreciative to Frank for his substantial contributions to this book and for the energetic flair and dedication he brings to our law partnership.

To all of the people at Shernoff, Bidart, Darras & Arkin who have been so gracious in giving me their continued support and time. I am particularly thankful to my law partner and writing and research genius, **Sharon Arkin**. To my terrific associate **Ricardo Echeverria,** and to my associates **Barbara Skier** and **Doug Carasso,** for their contribution, assistance, and encouragement.

To my assistants **Avril Haemmerle** and **Donna Newcomb,** who put up with me through this book-writing experience and showed incredible patience.

To all my clients and fellow trial lawyers who know what it is all about when it comes to FIGHTING BACK AND WINNING. They know more than anyone the ups and downs of fighting HMOs and insurance companies and the sacrifices it takes to meet the task of leveling the playing field.

An unidentified man screams after unfurling a banner accusing HMOs of being "in it for the money" moments before committing suicide April 30, 1998, on a Los Angeles freeway.
(AP Photo/courtesy KTLA)

INTRODUCTION

No event dramatized the plight of health care patients across America more than what occurred on Thursday, April 30, 1998, on a busy Los Angeles freeway. Newspaper headlines broadcast the shocking news to a national audience: **Suicide On The 110—HMO Protest Comes To A Deadly End**. As rush-hour traffic sat eerily still, unable to proceed because of police activity, a distraught man set himself on fire and then shot himself to death on live television after unfurling a banner that read, "HMOs are in it for the money."

Is our health care system willing to deny potentially life-saving care to the sickest of patients because turning a profit is more important than helping heal the sick?

No doubt about it! The health care system in this country needs fixing. But until the repairman comes, consumers must struggle through the confusing maze of what is presently available through HMOs and health insurers.

With more than 80% of Americans receiving their health insurance through their employers, consumers have few choices regarding their health care coverage. By the late 1970s, extraordinary health care inflation spawned a new type of health insurance called managed care. To control their runaway health insurance costs, employers predictably flocked to the new managed care companies that promised comprehensive medical care at lower group rates. Today, managed care is the dominant player in the health care industry, and consumers are the pawns. They've been pushed into managed care plans by a powerful insurance lobby that has successfully manipulated public opinion into believing that higher health care costs would likely lead employers to decide they cannot or will not provide health care benefits to their employees.

But more than ever, evidence supports the contention that managed health care providers care more about healthy profits than healthy people. Slick company brochures promise customers "peace of mind," "high quality health care options," and sympathetic members of a medical team who will "be there when you need them." But the reality is a health care system that cares more about the bottom line than providing the best possible medical care. We've all heard the horror stories of doctors who receive financial incentives to reduce or deny care, patients who can't get referrals to the specialists they need, and insurers that refuse to pay for emergency treatment at a hospital that doesn't belong to the HMO network.

Recent surveys indicate overwhelming public support for Congress to pass reform legislation to protect patients from managed care abuses and to hold managed care organizations accountable when their decisions hurt people. More than ever, consumers view managed care as a threat to quality health care. And they worry that their health care coverage won't be there when they need it most.

To understand the managed care industry, one must first realize that HMOs are profit-driven businesses that work on a system called "capitation." Under this arrangement, HMOs receive a flat fee per patient annually to provide for all of the member's medical needs. If the patient requires only routine, preventive care, the HMO stands to make a profit. But if the patient requires specialized care, and that care exceeds the agreed upon flat rate, HMOs and their doctors lose money.

As in all business, the quickest way to a good bottom line is to reduce services. HMOs are no different. They are constantly looking for ways to cut costs and avoid expenses. They reap profits by denying and reducing medically necessary care and aggressively limiting access to expensive procedures—all at the patients' expense. Even doctors and administrators may have an incentive to deny needed care because their financial well-being may be tied indirectly to providing the lowest possible level of care.

As if lowering costs at the expense of quality health care weren't bad enough, consumers have little legal recourse if their managed care company commits malpractice which causes injury—or even death—to their patients. The Employee Retirement Income Security Act of 1974 (ERISA) bars more than 150 million Americans with employer-provided health care from suing HMOs for damages no matter how terrible or brazen the malpractice. No other industry enjoys such protection from liability. With no penalty and no retribution, there is no incentive for managed care companies to make the right decisions on behalf of their patients. Managed care companies must be held accountable for their medical negligence, and the only way to do that is by giving patients the right to sue. Health care reform *must* include the right to sue because the threat of a potential lawsuit is the only way to deter managed care providers from running every medical decision through a financial filter.

HMO oversight by state authorities is weak—often nonexistent. Unless consumers are experts in the ins and outs of HMOs and traditional health insurance companies, they are in no better position than navigating their way through a minefield.

As a lawyer and a consumer advocate with more than 25 years of experience in insurance matters, I want to help consumers learn how they can help themselves. There is nothing more important than your good health and that of your loved ones. Knowledge is power, especially when it comes to making the tough decisions concerning your well-being. It is the intent of this book to empower the reader so that you can fight HMOs and win if the need arises.

Ordinary people can fight back and win. But it's a battle that must be fought publicly—in the courts, in the press, and in the legislative assemblies.

CHAPTER 1

How to get your hmo to pay up

People often assume that once they join a health maintenance organization (HMO), filing medical claims will be streamlined and trouble-free.

In fact, when it comes to delaying payment of benefits and denying legitimate claims, HMOs are no different than conventional fee-for-service health insurers.

HMO members usually pay a flat monthly fee (or share the fee paid by their employers) for medical care, regardless of how much or how little care they need. HMO doctors are usually paid a fixed monthly fee per patient—

called a "capitation" agreement—regardless of how much care they deliver.

This arrangement usually works well for simple diagnostic and preventive services. But in cases involving costly or experimental treatment, HMOs may be less likely than conventional insurers to make prompt reimbursement or authorize needed treatment.

Under the fast-disappearing fee-for-service relationship, a physician treats a patient and receives an agreed-upon fee for the service from the health insurer with, perhaps, a contribution from the patient. But the managed-care "package" is profit-driven, and, its managers are always looking for ways to cut costs and avoid expenses. Unfortunately, in today's climate, doctors and administrators may have an incentive to deny you the care you need because their financial well-being may be tied indirectly to giving you the lowest possible level of care.

Here's how to protect your interests—and what to do if your HMO refuses to pay your claims or provide necessary treatment.

BEFORE YOU SIGN UP

Check out the HMO's reputation. If your employer has contracted with an HMO, you may have little choice regarding your health insurance. *But if you do have a choice:* Contact the agency that oversees HMOs in your state (typically the Department of Insurance or the Department of

Corporations.) Inquire about the HMO's track record, including its history of complaints from consumers. If there are numerous complaints on record, find another insurer. You should also contact your state medical board and the American Medical Association to review doctors in the HMO network.

Other resources that can assist you in selecting a health insurer are the National Committee for Quality Assurance (*phone:* 202-955-3500; *web site:* http://www.ncqa.org), the Joint Commission on Accreditation of Healthcare Organizations (*phone:* 630-792-5800; *web site:* http://www.jcaho.org) and Pacific Business Group on Health (*phone:* 888-244-2124; *web site:* http://www.healthscope.org). Each of these organizations publishes ratings guides to the nation's HMOs, doctors, and nursing homes.

The art of beating your insurance company begins when you buy your policy. Specify what you want to be covered for and ask the customer service agent several "what-if" questions to get a sense of how your HMO will respond to difficult medical situations. Look for a plan that covers anticipated health needs, including alternative therapies such as acupuncture if that's what you prefer.

> • **Review carefully the list of doctors who participate in the HMO.** The more doctors on staff in the HMO's network, the less likely you'll be saddled with a doctor you don't like. *Also:* The more cardiologists, oncologists, and other medical specialists on the roster, the better. Keep in

mind that you have the right to change your primary care physician at any time for any reason.

- **Ask specifically if the HMO will allow you to get second opinions.** Enroll in an HMO that will permit you to get a second opinion if you request one. Be prepared to pay on your own if you go outside the HMO network.

- **Investigate how your HMO pays for catastrophic care.** Some HMOs are unwilling to pay for bone-marrow transplants and other costly—but lifesaving—treatments. Some are reluctant to pay for emergency care rendered to members when they're out of town. More recently, some HMOs have established "confinement" provisions that forbid a pregnant woman from receiving reimbursement for a medical emergency if she travels outside the HMO network's boundaries during her third trimester. To get a sense of how strict the HMO you're considering will be in evaluating your claims, ask how it would handle these situations.

- **Find out who is responsible for making difficult medical decisions.** The best HMOs let their *doctors* decide which tests are necessary, how long a patient should be hospitalized, whether a specialist must be called in, etc. Steer clear of HMOs that hire managed-care companies to perform this task. Many HMO administrators can overrule a doctor's opinion without ever examining the injured patient. Be sure to find out specifically how complaints will be handled if there is a dispute about care. *Best:* An HMO that has put in writing its procedures for handling disputes. Many HMOs have committees that review member complaints. If your HMO handles complaints this way, ask who runs the committee, whether there are doctors and administrators on the panel, and if there is a member/patient representative. Steer clear of HMOs that give health plan administrators the final decision over day-to-day operations.

AFTER SIGNING UP

Take an active role in the claims-filing process. With conventional fee-for-service, or pay-as-you-go health insurance, patients are responsible for filing their own claims. HMOs handle these claims for their patients in the network, sending their members a monthly statement of benefits paid only if outside services are required.

Like all insurers, HMOs insist that claims be filed in a certain way. If anything is wrong—a missing or improperly filled-out form, for example—the HMO is liable to deny the claim...or at least delay payment until the matter is cleared up. Be prepared for lengthy delays and bureaucratic nit-picking if there is a dispute.

While this arrangement works well for routine care, it can work against you in the event of a complex claim.

Self-defense: Ask the HMO to send you copies of all claims filed on your behalf. Review them, and see that any missing information is promptly provided to the HMO's home office. Keep copies of all documentation submitted with your claim.

> • **Create a paper trail.** If your HMO doctor is reluctant to order a costly or experimental test or procedure that you're convinced you need, get a second opinion. If this outside doctor agrees with you, ask him/her to write to the HMO on your behalf.

If you feel that your HMO doctor isn't doing all that he can do to ensure that the procedure is covered, contact the member services department of your HMO to register a complaint.

Your aim: To establish a written record that supports your case. This will come in handy should you need to appeal the denial of a claim or take the HMO to court.

IF YOUR CLAIM OR REQUEST IS DENIED

File an immediate appeal. Be sure to follow your insurer's complaint procedure outlined in your HMO handbook very carefully. Most health care companies require you to report your grievance to a specified person or department. Be sure to put your complaint in writing, include all relevant documentation to support your claim, and keep copies of everything.

Always state what action you want your HMO to take. And in each letter you write regarding your appeal, explain why you feel your benefits were wrongfully denied. Include the following sentence: *This appeal relates only to the denial of the benefits in question, but does not constitute, and shall in no way be deemed, an admission that I am limited in my right to pursue a "bad faith" remedy in state court.*

Communicate with the HMO by registered mail—even if you are not required to do so. Be sure to request a written response within 30 days.

Set up a folder for all the paperwork on the grievance and track on a calendar each step and when responses are due.

The HMO's first response to your appeal will probably be to reiterate the denial of your claim. Don't let that discourage you. Go on to the next step in the appeals process. Keep pursuing the matter until you've exhausted all the remedies outlined in the booklet. If the dispute is not settled by then, it will probably be referred to a third party for mediation and/or arbitration under the terms of your membership agreement.

Fact: You have the right to elect to go straight to arbitration, bypassing the HMO's formal appeal and grievance procedures. The internal appeal procedures set up by HMOs are not as independent as they claim. They are biased in favor of the health plan because managers in the

HMO's member services department are not likely to over-rule one of their own. The faster you can get your appeal heard before a truly independent third party, the better.

Claims most commonly denied: The two most commonly denied claims are for long-term skilled nursing care and durable medical equipment. Health plan administrators frequently deny costly skilled nursing care such as physical therapy, wound therapy, and feeding tube assistance. Instead, patients are told they require only "custodial" care that a family member or friend could administer. With regard to durable medical equipment, insurers often opt for supplying the lowest level of equipment—a rigid foot prosthetic rather than a flexible one, for example. Other claims that are frequently denied are bone-marrow transplants for metastatic breast cancer and other treatments the HMO deems "experimental" or "not medically necessary."

- **Let the HMO know that you mean business.** The HMO's "administrative remedy" is not your only remedy—and it's very important that the HMO knows you know that. That is why every letter you write should include the sentence that you reserve the right to go to state court. Another tactic to use against your HMO is to demand that you be allowed to be present for any review process.

- **File a complaint with the state.** If the appeals process proves futile, contact the appropriate state regulatory agency (the Department of Insurance or the Department of Corporations) and ask about the procedure for filing a formal complaint against the HMO. Many states have waiting periods, but in some emergency cases, a complaint may be filed immediately and heard within 72 hours. The department's decision, while influential, is not binding and you may be back to where you started. Always be sure to include a copy of your original complaint and all relevant correspondence.

Expect your claim to take anywhere from a month to a year to process. Most states receive a large number of complaints and lack the staff to deal with them in a timely fashion. But filing this complaint will extend the paper trail—a good strategy if it ultimately becomes necessary to file a lawsuit. You may also want to report cases of severe bad faith or fraudulent behavior to your state attorney general and/or local Better Business Bureau.

- **Make as much noise as possible.** Since state regulatory oversight in these areas is often weak, you may improve your chances by also reporting your problem to local consumer hotlines and consumer affairs reporters at television stations and newspapers.

- **Seek legal redress if necessary.** If the sum in dispute is small, you may be wiser to sue in small claims court. Check your state limits to see if this solution will work for you.

- **Hire a lawyer who specializes in "bad faith" insurance on behalf of plaintiffs.** An insurer that refuses to honor your valid claim under the terms of your policy without proper cause may be liable for "bad faith"—defined as a denial of benefits without reasonable cause. If the HMO has acted in bad faith, it may be liable for punitive or emotional distress damages as well as the benefits due under the insurance policy.

Limitation: If you joined the HMO through your employer, you're probably entitled to sue only for the cost of the denied treatment and attorneys' fees, and not for emotional distress, punitive damages, and other consequential damages as a result of the unfair denial.

You are better off hiring an attorney who specializes in insurance bad faith on a contingency basis (usually one-third of the amount recovered) so you'll be charged only if you win your case. If you need a referral, contact your state or local bar association. Also, it's a good idea to find out whether your state permits arbitration awards greater than your contested medical claims. If it does, that should increase your chances of finding a lawyer to represent you.

FOR PROBLEMS SPECIFIC TO MEDICARE CLAIMS, SEE CHAPTER 8.

LEGAL TIPS TO FOLLOW IF YOUR CLAIM IS DENIED

- ► Insist on a written explanation of your denial.

- ► Create a paper trail. Always keep accurate and thorough records of all names of people you talk to, and copies of all correspondence.

- ► Telephone the member claims examiner or adjuster who is assigned to your claim to question any decision you believe is unfair. Don't be afraid to contact the adjuster's supervisor, moving up the chain of command.

- ► File an immediate appeal. Follow your health plan's grievance procedure.

- ► Always follow up a phone conversation with a letter stating your complaint again. State your full name, include your member I.D. number, copies of bills, test results, doctor's statements, etc. Clearly state what action you want your HMO to take and request a written response within 30 days. In all your correspondence, include the sentence: This appeal relates only to the denial of the benefits in question, but does not constitute, and shall in no way be deemed, an admission that I am limited in my right to pursue a "bad faith" remedy in state court.

- ► Always communicate with your HMO by registered mail.

- ► Ask your doctor to call or write the HMO on your behalf.

- ► Get a second or third opinion from a qualified professional outside the HMO network.

- ► File a complaint with your state regulators (the Department of Insurance or Department of Corporations). Be sure to include copies of all correspondence between you and your HMO. Let your HMO know that you are contacting the state regulator about your problem.

- ► Enlist the help of consumer organizations, the media, and your state and federal elected officials. Write letters stating why you think you've been wronged.

- ► File a complaint with your state's medical board if you think your physician is withholding treatment for his/her own financial gain.

- ► If you receive your health insurance through your employer, notify the company's human resources department about your dissatisfaction with the plan. Enlist your group policy administrator at work for support.

- ► Hire a "bad faith" lawyer on a contingency fee basis, if necessary.

- ► Consider small claims court if the dispute is under your state's limit.

- ► Never give up! Managed care companies are counting on you to passively accept their decisions, even if they are wrong. Be persistent!

CHAPTER 2

BOTHERSOME HMO TRAPS TO WATCH OUT FOR

As an attorney who represents consumers who are trying to force health insurance companies to make good on their claims, I have recently noticed several disturbing trends in the ways managed-care providers and HMOs are denying or limiting payments to patients.

Here's what is worrying me most—and how to fight back.

- **Increase of bonus incentives.** A growing number of HMOs and managed-care systems give doctors, administrators, and claims adjusters financial incentives to deny or cut back coverage to their customers. To make intelligent decisions about health plans and health care options, it is critical that patients have access to as much information as possible about whether or not their doctors may be entitled to financial rewards for limiting patient care.

Unfortunately, insurance companies seldom disclose these financial arrangements to customers, except when disputes turn into lawsuits. Nevertheless, doctors are supposed to disclose any financial incentives for limited services, if asked.

- **Hidden arbitration clauses in plan documents.** Most people don't realize it, but when they sign up for coverage through some plans, they may abandon their constitutional right to a jury trial in the event of a health care policy dispute or fraudulent business practice.

Instead, they may have unwittingly agreed to file an *arbitration suit*, which is typically decided by administrative panels with strong ties to the medical community. In many states, these panels cannot award consumers more than the cost of the contested medical services.

It used to be that going to arbitration would expedite your complaint, but no longer. Mandatory arbitration proceedings have become a delaying tactic for many HMOs. It's very possible that electing to go to arbitration rather

than to trial (when you have a choice) may actually length-
en the appeals process and offer no remedy beyond the cost
of the denied treatment.

> • **HMOs may discourage doctors from referring
> patients to specialists.** I've encountered this
> problem often in cases when consumers require
> treatment that is expensive or somewhat new or
> unusual.

Typical problem areas: High-risk pregnancies...can-
cers...multiple sclerosis...and other serious chronic diseases.

Some HMOs and managed-care systems deny full
reimbursement to primary care physicians who refer
patients to specialists, no matter how severe the patients'
illnesses. I've seen other cases where the HMO has limited
the specialist's examination to one part of the body—the
knee only, for example, when the patient complained of hip
pain that might require hip surgery.

In the HMO setting, primary care physicians lose
money when they recommend specialists whose care
exceeds the primary care doctor's fixed pool of money for
their patients. This arrangement leads to an ethical conflict
that their patients only learn about if they sue the health
care provider.

Solution: The best thing you can do under these circumstances is complain. Start by making an argument in writing to your primary care physician about why you believe you

15

need a specialist's care. The next step is to complain to your HMO's board of directors. If the board isn't sympathetic, consider consulting a specialist on your own and filing your claim, and hope for the best. Your health always comes first.

- **Insurers may discourage doctors from recommending acute rehabilitation care.** Based upon my experience, this problem typically occurs among patients over age 65 following a serious stroke, serious injury that results in paraplegia or quadriplegia, or hip surgery.

Although the problem is widespread, it's most pronounced when Medicare patients receive their care from HMOs.

Solution: Don't succumb to the marketing pitches you hear from HMOs. There's absolutely no reason to assign your Medicare coverage to an HMO—you'll only wind up limiting your freedom of medical choice.

- **Insurers may refuse to pay for certain emergency treatments.** This usually happens when an HMO patient has a medical emergency while traveling and must be treated at a hospital that doesn't belong to the HMO network. It's also common in states where people work more than one hour from their homes and must seek treatment at non-member hospitals.

Trap: Providers often deny claims on the grounds that the patient should have been treated at his/her own hospital or could have been transferred to a member hospital.

Solution: Always request a letter from the emergency room facility documenting that you experienced a medical emergency and were unable to be transferred to another facility without endangering your health.

"Is there a doctor in the house affiliated with this person's HMO?"
©1998, Reprinted Courtesy of Bunny Hoest and Parade

17

HMO ABUSES MOST LIKELY TO LEAD TO A LAWSUIT

If you've seen the movie *As Good As It Gets*, you haven't likely forgotten the scene when an enraged Helen Hunt lashes out at the HMO industry for caring more about money than her son's health. Audiences cheered all across America.

My law firm receives hundreds of phone calls each month from consumers who are experiencing their own medical crises. Many have been wrongfully denied the medical treatment they deserve.

While we can't take on every case, we have noticed several disturbing patterns of abuse. When consumers wind up in court over a dispute, it is very likely to be because of one of these six HMO practices.

▶ *Case management by accountants.* Doctors' treatment decisions are routinely overruled by managed care bureaucrats on HMO payrolls who see only the number at the bottom line.

▶ *Denials of skilled nursing care.* Seniors are frequently denied the specialized nursing care that only a nursing facility can provide. Instead, managed care providers insist that these patients need only basic "custodial" care.

▶ *Limiting/delaying referrals to specialists.* Not only do some HMOs make it difficult to see a specialist, but some control or limit the parameters of the examination. Referrals to specialists sometimes take months—months that a sick patient may not have.

▶ *Restricting necessary medical equipment.* HMO patients often receive the lowest level of durable medical equipment. For example, the patient may require a walker and a wheelchair, but receive only a walker.

▶ *Denials of medical emergencies.* Expect a protracted struggle if you experience a medical emergency outside your HMO network. Insurers frequently deny claims on the grounds that the patient should have or could have been treated at his/her own member hospital.

▶ *Restricting care for seniors.* Medicare recipients who join an HMO are often denied routine advanced therapy, such as proton beam therapy for prostate cancer. When the care gets too expensive, the HMO drops the senior, transferring the costs back to the taxpayers.

CHAPTER 3

PRACTICAL TIPS TO FOLLOW SO THAT YOU DON'T END UP IN AN HMO DISPUTE

Many employers have been putting pressure on health insurers to cut their premiums. In turn, some insurance companies have grown increasingly ruthless—sometimes even unscrupulous—when it comes to paying out for their policyholders. What you should know about health insurance to reduce the chances that you and your family end up in a health insurance dispute...

- **Avoid switching health insurance plans.** If you have coverage with which you are happy, avoid changing health care insurers, especially if you have a chronic medical condition or have had a recent health problem. *Reason:* A new insurer will almost certainly exclude coverage for any "pre-existing" condition and may find you "uninsurable" if your medical problem is serious. Even if your health is good, many insurers impose waiting periods on new policyholders for certain procedures. *Exception:* If your employer changes insurers, most state insurance laws require that the new insurer provide the same coverage without penalty to you.

- **Avoid temporarily dropping out of a health plan.** Many companies offer an annual "menu" of benefits from which to choose: health and life insurance, paid vacation days, child-care and retirement contributions, etc. Healthy employees or those who are included on a spouse's policy are often tempted to forego temporarily the medical plan in favor of other benefits.

Catch: Even if your company tells you otherwise, the insurance company is not obligated to take you back as an individual after you waive the group medical benefits. Even if you provide evidence of your insurability, your coverage may be denied or restricted.

- **Don't drop your family coverage either...for the same reason.** Many companies offer financial incentives to employees who waive family coverage. While at first it may not make sense to pay for double coverage when both spouses work, it is always a gamble to drop coverage. Should the insured spouse die, lose his/her job, or the couple divorce, the family could find itself uninsured. In cases of serious illness or injury, the double coverage will be welcome.

- **Choose "household name" insurers.** Always select a large, well-established insurer. Large insurance companies have more experience dealing with specialized care and the volume of a managed care network.

- **Beware of policies that exclude coverage if you become eligible for Medicare.**

Catch: Anyone who is disabled by a catastrophic illness or injury becomes Medicare-eligible. Insurers would like to shift the cost of catastrophic care to the taxpayer. But you are paying premiums to ensure better protection than Medicare can provide in case of crisis. Look for a policy that pays costs "over and above" what Medicare will pay.

- **Contact your federal representatives and ask them to close the ERISA loophole. (See Chapter 11 for a discussion on ERISA, the 1974 federal law that governs group health plans.)**

Copley News Service/Michael Ramirez

CHAPTER 4

INSURANCE TRAPS THAT CAN EFFECTIVELY CANCEL YOUR COVERAGE

WHAT TO WATCH FOR...WHAT TO AVOID

Exclusions are the clauses in your insurance contract that eliminate coverage you may believe you've been paying for. It is very important to read the list of explicit exclusions that appears in every insurance policy.

If you are dissatisfied, ask your insurance agent to propose alternatives.

Example: If there is a history of alcoholism or depression in your family and your medical policy excludes coverage for substance abuse or psychiatric treatment, you may want to buy supplemental coverage or change policies.

Health insurance policies are particularly tricky. Often, exceptions to coverage are camouflaged within other sections of the policy and are not reflected in the exclusions section at all. These are the most problematic exclusions and "camouflaged exclusions" to watch for.

HEALTH INSURANCE EXCLUSIONS TRAPS

- *Custodial care exclusion:* This clause is intended to exclude coverage for nursing homes, residences for the mentally or physically disabled, or other facilities of a custodial rather than a medical nature.

Whenever possible, insurers will reduce the number of skilled nursing days a patient may be eligible for, and categorize the level of care required as custodial in nature to reduce their own financial burden.

Trap: Insurers have begun to invoke the custodial care exclusion in cases of catastrophic accidents or illnesses when the patient is not expected to recover but requires intensive care, life support equipment such as a respirator, or other costly measures. Insurers are claiming that because the patient is not expected to benefit from treatment, the care is "custodial" and therefore not covered.

Recourse: These denials are being successfully fought by policyholders in court. Legally, the "reasonable expectations" of the policyholder prevail in cases where insurance policy language is unclear or open to interpretation. Ask your doctor to order skilled nursing care. If it is denied, ask who denied it and how the decision was reached. Always get everything in writing.

- *Experimental treatment exclusion:* This clause is being invoked by insurers to exclude very costly procedures—including bone-marrow transplants for cancer patients, even though the procedure is considered standard by the American Medical Association.

Caution: Some insurance companies deny payment for such procedures, even if the exclusion does not appear in the policy, by claiming that they are experimental and therefore not "medical" treatment.

Trap: Insurance companies are generally getting away with such denials of claims unless they are taken to court.

Recourse: If your claim is denied the first time, have your doctor write the insurer, citing evidence for the medical acceptability of the treatment. If you are turned down a second time, see a lawyer.

CAMOUFLAGED HEALTH INSURANCE TRAPS

- **Definitions section.** Narrow definitions can drastically limit coverage.

Example: A policy promising hospital coverage that defines "hospital" as an "acute care facility" may effectively exclude extended care facilities and rehabilitation hospitals even though these types of facilities are not specifically excluded.

- **Limits of liability.** Check how much your policy will pay for a hospital stay or a specific procedure, then compare your findings with charges by typical hospitals or physicians in your area. Is there a cap on prescription drug payments? Does coverage start on the first day of hospitalization?

Trap: Some hospital indemnity policies pay a flat rate for every hospital day, starting on the seventh day, excluding extended care and rehabilitation facilities. If you are injured in an accident, spend a week in the hospital, and are transferred to a rehab facility thereafter, you could get nothing.

Another common trap is the "qualifying stay provision," which requires Medicare patients to spend three days in an acute care facility before they become eligible for skilled nursing care. A patient discharged from the hospital after just two days won't qualify for any skilled nursing care regardless of the physician's orders.

- *Major medical policies that pay "hospital charges."* You might assume that your treatment for cancer would be covered under a major medical policy.

Trap: You may find that 90% of you treatment is excluded if you receive chemotherapy as an outpatient, as is common practice. Check the wording of your policy!

- **Medical necessity.** Whether it is implied or specifically stated in the policy, some insurers have denied claims on the grounds that the procedure of hospitalization is "not medically necessary." Don't forget, these denials are often made by managed care bureau-crats who have never even examined the patient!

Example: One of my clients had symptoms of a life-threatening condition. His physician ordered him hospital-ized, where tests proved negative. His insurer then refused coverage, claiming the tests could have been done on an outpatient basis, so the hospitalization wasn't medically necessary. *Result:* The insurer lost in court.

Your physician, not your insurance company, has the right to determine what is medically necessary, unless the company can show the doctor has acted contrary to accept-ed medical practice.

Recourse: Have treatment "pre-authorized" whenever possible. Insurers are much less likely to deny coverage for treatment they have judged "reasonable" ahead of time.

You can improve your chances of a successful out-come by establishing a personal relationship with the case manager in charge of your care. As a member, you have a right to see what the case manager has written on your chart and what has been recommended to your physician. When HMO employees know you're taking a proactive approach to your care, they are less likely to put up roadblocks.

- **Reasonable and customary charges.** Many policies cover 80% of charges they deem to be "reasonable and customary." Your doctor may charge $5,000 for an operation, but your insurer may only want to pay 80% or $4,000.

Trap: Insurance companies are known to use outdated fee schedules and to average rates that may not reflect what is "reasonable and customary" in your area.

Recourse: Canvas the doctors in your area to show that the fee is reasonable, and challenge the decision. Ask the doctors for a breakdown of "reasonable and customary" fees for your particular procedure. These fee schedules are usually referred to as a "Relative Value Scale."

- **Medicare eligibility.** Many insurers bury a phrase somewhere in their policies stating that they exclude coverage if the policyholder becomes Medicare-eligible.

Trap: Anyone who is disabled by a catastrophic illness or accident and can no longer work is eligible for Medicare. The intent of this phrase is to shift the burden of paying for catastrophic care to the taxpayers. But policyholders faithfully pay premiums to private insurers to guarantee that they won't have to depend on Medicare alone, and will have access to the highest-quality care in the case of lengthy or disabling illness.

Caution: Look for a policy that doesn't cancel payments if you become eligible for Medicare. If you already have a policy that cancels coverage, you should definitely contest that once you're eligible for Medicare since it is really not a catastrophic policy—and may have been misrepresented as such.

WHAT YOUR INSURANCE COMPANY WON'T TELL YOU

Myth: Insurance companies deliberately write policies that are difficult to understand, then interpret the language to their own benefit, leaving you out in the cold.

Reality: Courts have held that when insurance policy language is unclear, the language will be construed against the insurance company. If your interpretation of the language is reasonable, you're likely to win.

Myth: Most claim denials are based on difficult to understand exclusionary language that is buried deep in your policy.

Reality: Courts have held that exclusions must be phrased in plain, clear language that the lay person can understand. Don't take no for an answer if you believe the exclusionary language is confusing or contradictory.

Myth: Failure to fill out an insurance form properly is a valid reason for a denial.

Reality: Not true. Technical deficiencies, including late filing, are no reason to deny a claim. Your insurance company has the burden of proof to show it has been harmed by your incomplete form(s). If it can't, technical problems can't be used to deny your claim.

Myth: Your insurance company can deny your claim without a written explanation.

Reality: All states require insurance companies to issue a written explanation when your claim is denied, usually within 30 days. Failure to do so may be an unfair claims practice. Consult your state Department of Insurance or a local consumer organization for more information.

Myth: Insurance companies can rely on their "master" insurance policy rather than the descriptive booklets that outline their coverage when interpreting policy language.

Reality: Your reasonable interpretation of the policy language may govern over the fine print in the master policy. Be sure to save insurance company brochures that outline your coverage.

Myth: Insurance companies don't have to respond to your complaint if they feel there has been no abuse.

Reality: An insurance company that does not respond to your complaint may be guilty of an unfair claims practice. Always be sure to include a deadline for their reply when corresponding with your managed care company.

CHAPTER 5

Hmo coverage in spite of pre-existing conditions

Your HMO policy is likely to exclude coverage for pre-existing conditions. Here's what you need to know to ensure that you receive all the care and treatment to which you are entitled.

GENERAL RULE

A "pre-existing condition" is a medical condition...

- for which you received medical help, AND

- which presented symptoms that a physician could have diagnosed with reasonable accuracy,
- during a specified period immediately *preceding* your health care policy's effective date.

Purpose of rule: To protect consumers from losing out on health benefits for a pre-existing condition of which he had no knowledge.

Objective standard: In some states, such as California, there is an "objective reasonableness" standard for when an illness or injury is first *manifest*. Under this standard, what determines whether the insured has coverage are the symptoms present that would or would not lead an average reasonable person to seek medical help. It is not the result or treatment of the condition that determines coverage.

Partial waiver of exclusion: Your HMO policy may *waive* the pre-existing condition exclusion up to a *maximum* amount.

Example: Before the policy's effective date, you had a condition for which an average reasonable person would have sought medical help. And you seek treatment for the same condition *after* your new policy has gone into effect. Your policy may partially waive the pre-existing condition exclusion by paying a *maximum benefit* of, say, $2,000 for this treatment. Any medical treatment of this condition costing more than $2,000 would not be covered, and must be paid for by you.

Conditions not subject to exclusion: Check your policy to see if there are certain medical conditions that are not subject to the pre-existing condition exclusion. The laws of your state may preclude this exclusion for certain conditions.

Under federal legislation enacted in 1996, HMOs may not impose the pre-existing condition exclusion to (1) newborns or adopted children applying within 30 days for coverage through employer-sponsored health plans; or (2) pregnancy.

KEY TIME PERIODS

For group health insurance plans, an HMO may impose a pre-existing condition exclusion only if it relates to a condition for which medical treatment should have reasonably been sought within, at most, the *6 months* immediately preceding enrollment in the health plan.

Under federal law, the exclusion may apply for no more than *12 months* after the effective date of coverage—although for late enrollees in the plan, this period is extended to 18 months.

For a direct-pay HMO policy covering only one or two people, the periods both before and after the effective dates are extended, to no more than *12 months*. It is absolutely essential that you determine from your policy what pre- and post-enrollment time periods apply to you.

Pre-enrollment period example: Suppose you sought medical help for an illness you had from June 15 to June 25. Your employer-provided group HMO plan took effect on December 26, the same date that an identical illness suddenly resurfaces. The policy provides that the pre-enrollment period covering the pre-existing condition exclusion is 6 months. Since more than 6 months have passed since your illness' previous appearance, you should not be denied coverage because of a pre-existing condition exclusion.

Post-enrollment period example: What if, instead, you had the illness from August 15 to August 28? The policy took effect on December 26. And the policy provides that the post-enrollment period covering the pre-existing condition exclusion is 6 months. But the illness doesn't reappear, and so you don't seek medical help until July 27 of the next year. Since over 6 months have passed, once again no pre-existing condition exclusion should deny you coverage.

Waiting period: Rather than an express exclusion for pre-existing conditions, some HMO policies provide for a waiting period or probationary period that applies to all injuries and illnesses. It is usually for 90 days. This provision precludes, over the specified period, coverage or benefits for any illness or injury that existed prior to the effective date of the policy.

New job: Suppose you (or your spouse or child) has a pre-existing condition, for which coverage is provided under an HMO or other health plan. You then start another job that provides, at no cost to you, health care coverage under a new HMO plan.

Dilemma: Should you continue under your present health plan or switch to the HMO offered by your new employer?

If you continue with your current health plan: You must pay the plan's monthly premiums. The new HMO would cost you nothing.

If you switch to the new HMO: You may fear that you (or your spouse or child) will not continue to receive coverage for the pre-existing condition.

In this situation, you must be mindful of the dates set forth in the policy as to when the condition must arise so as to constitute a precluded "pre-existing condition" and for how long after the policy's effective date such coverage is excluded.

EMPLOYER CHANGES HEALTH PLANS

The employer that provides you with health care coverage with HMO Plan ABC coverage may replace it with HMO Plan XYZ. And the new plan may deny coverage for an injury or sickness for which you did consult or should have consulted a doctor within the appropriate period before the new policy begins.

Danger: The medical expenses you incur for obtaining treatment for your prior condition may be denied by HMO Plan XYZ as an excluded "pre-existing condition."

Protection: The policy itself may waive the exclusion up to a maximum benefits amount. More importantly, the insurance law of your state (as is the case in California) may preclude any exclusion of a "pre-existing condition" by a subsequent HMO plan for a condition covered under an employer's previously provided HMO plan.

Caution: If you continue to receive coverage for treatment of your pre-existing condition, you should also consider one more factor: Your doctors. You may be treated by specialists whom you wish to continue treating you—but who are not on HMO Plan XYZ's approved list of providers. Short of negotiating for HMO Plan XYZ's express approval for you to continue treatment with these out-of-plan specialists, you may prefer to continue with HMO Plan ABC on an individual or direct-pay basis, which would require you to pay the premiums. This is a choice that you and your pocketbook have to make.

INDIVIDUAL SWITCH FROM ONE HMO TO ANOTHER

You may have on your own obtained health care coverage for yourself or both yourself and your dependents. Before switching to an HMO or to a new HMO, read the policy of this prospective HMO to see what pre-existing conditions—and at what times they must be manifest—are precluded from coverage.

Important: Be aware of when you developed any unusual symptoms, as well as any medical advice, diagnosis, care, or treatment that you sought as a result.

Remember: It is the timing of these symptoms—and not your ultimate treatment or result—that determines when your condition first manifested and thus became a "pre-existing condition."

MEDICARE CONCERNS

Medicare beneficiaries are entitled to receive coverage for all benefits provided by the HMO—regardless of whether they relate to any "pre-existing condition"—with only two exceptions:

- End-Stage Renal Disease Care and Treatment (for when the patient is on dialysis), and
- Hospice Care for Terminally Ill Patients

Whatever your circumstances, the best rule of thumb is to be honest and truthful when documenting pre-existing medical conditions. A false claim is likely to go unpaid.

CHAPTER 6

TRAPS IN COMPANY-PROVIDED DISABILITY INSURANCE...

HOW TO PROTECT YOURSELF

For most employees, disability insurance is something the company may provide, few workers have enough of, and no one understands. After all, none of us likes to think about an extended sickness or traumatic injury that would prevent us from gassing up our cars, putting food on our tables, and clothing our loved ones. But disability does happen and always without warning, so you need to be prepared.

SHORT-TERM DISABILITY INSURANCE

Short-term disability coverage is just that—short-term. It usually lasts from 13 to 26 weeks. Benefits begin after a very short waiting period—zero to seven days—if you can't perform the substantial and material duties of your job. During the waiting period or elimination period, you don't get any money.

Example: Typically, a company's short-term disability policy pays 60 to 70 percent of your monthly salary. If you make $2000 a month and your short-term disability policy pays a 60% benefit, your monthly benefit would be $1200.

Trap: You are required to pay taxes on the benefits you receive if your company pays all the premiums for your short-term disability coverage.

Tip: Investigate if your employer will allow you to pay all or part of your short-term coverage. If you are permitted to contribute to your short-term coverage, your benefits will be tax-free. For example, if your monthly benefit is $1200 and you pay 50% of the premium, then one-half of the benefits will be taxable and the other half will be tax-free.

Also, ask your Human Resources department or benefits administrator if you can increase your coverage by paying the difference. If the company offers a 50% benefit, for instance, you may be able to increase your coverage to 70% by paying the difference yourself.

Key: Determine what definition of "disability" your insurance company will use to determine whether you are disabled under a short-term disability policy.

Most insurers will cover an accident or illness that prevents a policyholder from performing the physical and mental duties of his job.

Self-defense: Review your company's description of your job duties. Be sure it accurately reflects all of the physical and mental requirements necessary to do your job. If it is inadequate, supplement your occupational description so that it accurately reflects the amount of standing, bending, lifting, squatting, climbing, walking, reaching, carrying and driving that you do. Be sure to include what kind of tools and equipment are necessary to do your work.

Tip: Be thorough when providing occupational information to your treating doctor. He will be required to certify your disability on a monthly basis and to evaluate physical and cognitive limitations that prevent you from doing your job.

Be honest about how you feel. Don't be a hero and put on a happy face when you feel lousy. Be sure to tell your doctor if you're experiencing dizziness, drowsiness, an upset stomach, or other side effects from your prescribed medications. If you don't tell your doctor about your problems, your insurance company won't learn about them either.

Trap: Some insurance companies may inform you during the claims process that policyholders may have only one disabling condition at a time. For example, if your back hurts and you're suffering from depression, your insurance company may tell you that it has to close one claim before it opens the second. *Don't fall for this!* Remember, you are insured for your whole body. Your insurer *must* consider *all* your claims for disability.

SURVEILLANCE VIDEOTAPE

Be careful when your doctor says "be as active as possible." Insurance companies love to secretly videotape policyholders who have a claim on file, then compare what they see with your alleged restrictions and limitations. If the monthly progress statement that you submit to your insurer along with your treating doctor's monthly certification are inconsistent with the activities on the videotape, a red flag is raised. If you aren't supposed to do heavy lifting or repetitive activity, don't do it. Be careful! Videotape is very powerful and can destroy your claim and your credibility.

Tips: Report to your local law enforcement all suspicious vans, trucks or cars prowling near your home.

Don't carry heavy luggage to your car or load your kids into their car seats. Have someone else drag your trash cans out to the curb. Don't exercise in public places. Spread out your "must do" errands over several days so you're not videotaped doing everything on your good day.

Be vigilant. Ask yourself if your activity is consistent with your doctors' restrictions and limitations and with what you listed on your monthly progress statement.

SHORT-TERM DISABILITY REQUIREMENTS

Don't be tempted to cut back to part-time status when you first become sick or injured. By cutting back to fewer than 30 hours per week, you could be jeopardizing all of your short-term disability benefits.

Some short-term disability policies require a policy-holder to be "actively employed" and working 30 hours per week just prior to claiming a disability. These "at-work" requirements are often hidden in the small print of your group certificate or policy booklet.

Tip: Be sure you have financial resources available for at least four months if your employer doesn't provide short-term disability coverage. You'll wait a long time before long-term disability kicks in.

LONG-TERM DISABILITY INSURANCE

Employer-provided long-term disability policies usually cover injuries or sickness after a 90- to 180-day waiting period if it has been determined that you are unable to perform the functions of *your* occupation for 24 months. After 24 months, the definition shifts to *any* occupation for which you are trained, educated, or suited.

Trap: After 24 months of disability, most carriers cut off benefits, and previous earnings are not taken into account. For example, a new car sales manager is disabled from his occupation making $100,000 a year. The carrier pays the first 24 months. After 24 months, the insurer may claim the policyholder can sell encyclopedias by phone and agrees only to pay benefits based on a salary of $25,000 a year.

Trap: Most group benefits are reduced or "off-set" by the amount of money you receive from state disability, workers' compensation, and social security—*even if you don't apply for them.* With these sweeping "off-sets," your long-term disability benefit can be as low as the "benefit minimum" of $50 a month.

Tips: Read your group certificate or policy booklet carefully to determine what "off-set" or "benefit reductions" your policy contains.

Save enough money to build up an emergency fund in the event that you become disabled. You won't become eligible for benefits until after the 180-day waiting period, and it could take up to 7½ months before your disability coverage kicks in.

COMPANY TRAPS

Unless you work for the state, federal, or local governments, a church, or a school district, your employer's long-term disability plan is regulated under the Employee Retirement Income Security Act (ERISA) guidelines. As a result, you and your family lose nearly all of your legal rights to sue if you do not receive the benefits to which you are entitled.

Under ERISA, you are not allowed to seek punitive damages or any other compensatory or consequential damages resulting from unfair or even fraudulent claims denials. You cannot sue your insurer for damages if it unfairly delays or denies your medical, life, or disability claim. Your only recourse is to take your insurer to federal court where your case would likely be decided within 15 months by a federal court judge, not by a jury.

If you lose your home in foreclosure because your insurer delayed paying your monthly benefit, your equity loss is not recoverable.

These restrictions seriously limit your ability to hire a lawyer—meaning that you're likely to have to pay for all legal services out of your own pocket.

ADMINISTRATIVE RECORD

Most ERISA cases will be decided on the "administrative record" that the policyholder, his employer, and treating physician submit to support the disability claim.

Don't assume the insurance company gathered all your medical records from your doctors. Some insurers only request "office" or "chart" notes. During the claim process, be sure to document and support your claim by sending...

- *All* occupational information that lists the important duties of your occupation.
- *All* medical records, including charts, test results, and progress notes that support your restrictions and limitations.

CHAPTER 7

THE RIGHT
DISABILITY
COVERAGE

E mployer-paid short- and long-term disability plans offer few legal safeguards, offer limited monthly benefits, and are generally taxable.

WHY INDIVIDUAL POLICIES MAKE SENSE

- Individually applied for and paid disability policies are yours to keep when you change jobs.
- Individual policies do *not* contain "off-set" provisions that reduce your monthly benefits like short- and long-term group plans.

- Your monthly benefit checks are not taxed since you're paying the annual premium.
- Individual policies generally are not subject to ERISA, and therefore offer greater consumer safeguards if your claim is unfairly delayed or denied.
- If you must sue to collect your benefits, your insurer can be held liable for punitive damages, emotional distress damages, and other consequential damages if, for instance, you lose your home as a result of the delay or denial.
- You'll be entitled to a trial by jury and attorney fees that were spent or incurred in collecting the contract benefits.

SHOPPING FOR A POLICY

You should always apply through and purchase your individual disability policy from a licensed and appointed insurance agent—not a broker. Agents provide the highest level of consumer safeguards. Agents who sell individual disability policies offer all the major insurance company products.

Trap: If you purchase a policy from a broker, *you're* responsible for any errors that appear on your application that may have been taken down erroneously. Mistakes or errors made by an agent are the responsibility of the insurance company. If you are unsure of your salesperson's status, check with your state Department of Insurance and request a list of the disability companies that have appointed him.

GREAT POLICY ESSENTIALS

Here are what I consider to be the best disability insurance policy features, *in order of their importance to consumers.* Choose as many as you can afford by comparing different features, advantages and benefits, and the financial standing of the insurance companies.

- **Own-occupation coverage** guarantees benefit payments if you are unable to perform the substantial and material duties of your job when you become disabled.

Example: If a heart surgeon with own-occupation coverage developed a hand tremor and could no longer safely operate but could work as a general practitioner, she would be considered totally disabled and would receive full monthly, tax-free benefits if she chose to work as a general practitioner.

Most carriers limit own-occupation coverage to age 65. Some offer only two or five years of own-occupation coverage, then the definition shifts to *any occupation* for which you are trained, educated, or suited.

Trap: Any-occupation coverage is cheaper, but it won't pay if you can work at any other job.

Example: If the same heart surgeon could teach in medical school, she would not be considered disabled or entitled to any further benefits under any-occupation coverage.

Tip: Shop around for own-occupation coverage that pays for the longest period of time that you can afford.

- **Non-cancellable-guaranteed-renewable coverage** means your insurance company cannot cancel, increase your premium, or change its contract language as long as you pay your premiums on time—even if the insurer no longer does business in your state.

Trap: Some carriers offer guaranteed renewable products, but their premiums can be adjusted to reflect the number of claims on file. Be sure to avoid this coverage!

- **Waiver of premium rider** requires the insurer to waive your premium payments for your disability insurance while you are disabled.
- **Waiting period of no more than 120 days (90 days is better)** for benefits to begin after you become totally or partially disabled.

Remember, benefits won't accrue until after the waiting period expires. With a 90 day waiting period, your first check won't arrive for 4½ months after your disability begins. The longer the waiting period, the cheaper the coverage, but you'll need to put more money aside in case of a disabling injury or illness.

- **Lifetime benefits** provide monthly payments for as long as you are alive and totally disabled. This valuable rider can add 20 percent to the premiums cost of your policy. But most insurers don't like to offer it.

Second best: Benefits that last until age 65 if you are unable to work at your own occupation.

Avoid "income loss" or "new replacement loss" policies that limit benefits to two years and require policyholders to perform work that the insurance company says you're able to do or provide no benefits at all.

- **Coverage for mental and nervous disorders beyond 24 months** is very desirable but nearly impossible to find.

Trap: If your back pain is causing your depression, be careful to document it that way. If you're claiming chronic fatigue or chronic pain, be sure your doctor is clear when he describes the physical problems that are causing your secondary depression. Complaints of depression are a red flag and most insurers stop all benefits after 24 months.

- **Cost of living adjustments** guarantee your monthly disability benefits will be adjusted annually to keep up with inflation. This option costs more, but it's worth it.

UNDERWRITING

Medical underwriting—or investigating—has gotten tougher over the last five years with blood, urine, and HIV testing. Before you sit down with a licensed and appointed agent, ask her to send you the medical portion of the application so you can accurately provide all "yes" answers with the proper diagnosis, dates of treatment, and duration of any sickness of injury you are disclosing. Be sure you have your doctor's name, address, and telephone numbers.

Tip: If you have had extensive or adverse health problems, ask your agent to submit a "trial application," to several insurance companies before you formally apply for coverage. This way, you'll know in advance whether or not you'll be covered.

Reason: By submitting a trial application, you can avoid having to respond yes to the question, "Have you ever been declined insurance coverage before?" If the insurance company indicates it won't issue coverage to you, wait several years, then resubmit a trial application until you can find coverage.

Tip: Ask your agent whether you need to fast for 12 hours before you have blood drawn. Many insurance companies "rate" or charge a higher premium if your blood work comes back abnormal. Sometimes just eating a small meal before your blood is drawn can adversely affect your blood results and cause higher premiums.

BOTTOM LINE

Negotiate for more monthly disability dollars when you apply for coverage by providing signed and accurate tax returns.

Don't try to save money on your annual premiums by accepting a *partial or residual benefit* option. These riders sound great: They will pay part of your benefits if you can perform one but not all of the duties of your occupation.

Problem: Residual riders are used by insurers to avoid their responsibility and payment of total disability benefits for which you paid. If you have such an option, the insurer will work hard to find one or more duties that you can perform. That means you will receive only a prorated part of your benefits rather than the full amount.

Better: Purchase a straight total disability policy without any residual option or rider. Make sure you document all of the substantial and material duties you're unable to perform at work as well as the physical and mental restrictions that prevent you from returning to your occupation.

OTHER INDIVIDUAL DISABILITY POLICIES TO CONSIDER

- **Mortgage disability insurance.** This policy will cover your monthly mortgage if you are unable to perform your occupation. It's available through your lender or from any reputable licensed and appointed insurance agent.

Trap: Most mortgage disability coverage provides own-occupation coverage for just 24 months, then shifts to any-occupation for which you are trained, educated or suited.

Tip: Negotiate for own-occupation coverage for the life of your home loan.

- **Credit card disability.** May be purchased from most major credit card companies. This type of policy will pay your monthly minimum balance on your credit cards if you are disabled. You will be protected for 18 months in your own-occupation, then the definition shifts to any-occupation.
- **Life insurance waiver of premium for disability.** Optional coverage you can purchase when you buy term, universal, or whole life insurance. This rider will pay your monthly life insurance premium if you're totally disabled from your own-occupation during the first 12 or 24 months of disability, then the definition switches to any-occupation.

BASIC GUIDELINES

- Shop around. Compare each insurance company's features, advantages, and benefits against competitors.
- Always purchase your coverage from a licensed and appointed agent rather than an insurance broker.
- Provide accurate medical records and tax returns.
- Negotiate for more monthly disability dollars by selecting the longest own-occupation coverage you can afford.

CHAPTER 8

HMO COVERAGE FOR MEDICARE RECIPIENTS

I f you are or will soon be 65 years old, Medicare is of immediate interest to you. Although Medicare is supposed to provide those 65 and up with some sense of security, adding an HMO to the mix requires seniors to be mindful and vigilant. Otherwise, they may not obtain all the health care benefits to which they are entitled, and which their life and health require.

THE FOUR TYPES OF MEDICARE COVERAGE PLANS:

(1) Traditional Medicare

- *Medicare Part A:* Provides for *Inpatient Hospitalized Services* and *Skilled Care*. Inpatient Hospitalized Services are covered without limitation based on *medical necessity*. Skilled Care, based on need, is provided by a skilled or certified professional up to 100 days per "benefit period"—which is defined as a 3-day qualifying stay in an acute hospital followed by placement in a skilled nursing facility. The patient who remains past the 100 days would then have to leave the skilled nursing facility for 60 consecutive days before a new benefit period would begin.

- *Required payment:* A senior must pay a deductible ($450 per year), as well as a percentage of fees (usually 20%, leaving Medicare to pay the remaining 80%).

- *Optional Medicare Part B:* This additional coverage provides for *Outpatient Care, Physician Office Visits*, and *Home Health Needs*. The Medicare recipient pays a monthly premium of about $38.

Caution: Some home health needs or supplies will not be covered under Part B. For example, a patient who requires suctioning and tracheotomy care in the home or a skilled nursing facility will not be provided a respiratory therapist to help with the suctioning and care of the tracheotomy. This will fall on less experienced health care providers, such as an aide in the skilled nursing facility or an available family member at home.

(2) Medicare Plus Medigap

"Medigap" policies are 10 standardized packages for private health insurance policies sold as supplements to Medicare. Medigap is provided to all Part B Medicare recipients. The federal government has standardized the policies and guaranteed that they are renewable.[1]

(3) Retirement Benefits

An employer may provide extra benefits to a retiree with supplemental insurance. This is similar to the Medigap program, but it is earned as part of the retirement. Still, this supplemental program fits under the provisions and limitations of ERISA. (See Chapter 11 for a discussion on ERISA.)

(4) HMOs

An increasing number of Medicare recipients have switched from fee-for-service health care to managed care plans—a large number of which are HMOs. These HMOs provide or arrange for all Medicare-covered services. They usually charge fixed monthly premiums and minimal copayments, and they provide additional benefits at little or no cost. HMOs charge their patients a premium, in advance, that covers nearly all medical care provided by the health care practitioners affiliated with each HMO.

[1] For further information, write to the National Association of Insurance Commissioners (NAIC) at Consumer Information Center, Department 59, Pueblo, Colorado 81009. Identify the information as "Guide to Health Insurance for People with Medicare" and the publication number 518-Y. You can also pick up a copy of this Guide at a district Social Security office, which will have information evaluating the contents and quality of specific policies under Medigap.

Beware of Deceptive Advertisements: HMOs have entered an arena of competition for senior citizen contracts. They sell their plans by setting up meetings, even parties called the "Pie Party Sell," offering free food and featuring celebrity support individuals, including those featured in its advertisements. The ads often depict seniors who ride bikes, trim roses, or dance ballet. They never address the senior who is in the hospital or the skilled nursing facility for long-term or catastrophic illness. This may be because when seniors are chronically ill or require expensive treatments, health plans often attempt to get the senior to disenroll and go back to traditional Medicare.

Example: A 72-year-old senior has difficulty urinating. His urologist performs tests and diagnoses prostate cancer. The urologist recommends a few treatment options, which include proton beam therapy.

The patient lives in an area in which proton beam therapy is provided. But the therapy costs about $20,000, and the health plan denies the treatment. The patient appeals through the HMO, and a second denial from the plan follows.

The patient then disenrolls and appeals through the Center for Health Dispute Resolution (CHDR), an ombudsman program set up by Medicare. Without success, the patient then appeals to the Administrative Law Justice, which reverses the Plan's decision and promises payment of the proton beam therapy.

Supplemental/Additional Coverage: HMO senior plans often contain supplemental or additional provisions such as pharmacy coverage or vision care that are not a part of the basic policy. It pays to look closely at such coverage. For example, one HMO plan provides $500 per year to cover your use of name-brand pharmaceuticals. But this HMO plan also offers "discount store" drugs if you agree to use its in-network pharmacy, whose drugs may have imperfections and possible side effects. What they tell you is that your $500 will go further because these lesser drugs are cheaper.

And if you want pharmaceuticals from this plan at no cost to you, you can send in your prescription to the mail order warehouse and obtain still lesser quality drugs, which have even *more* undisclosed imperfections and potential side effects.

PROBLEMS SPECIFIC TO MEDICARE CLAIMS

The over-utilization of Medicare funds in the past was astounding. Physicians were referring patients to their own facilities for outpatient procedures that were paid for by Medicare. This referring system was not monitored and served the physician's rather than the patient's needs.

The federal government aggressively resolved the difficulties caused by over-utilization of tests and procedures by introducing the Medicare Risk Program that certified HMOs to provide "capitation" programs in which the federal government would be able to pre-pay a monthly fixed fee to the HMO for each patient.

The pendulum has now swung to under-utilization practices for HMOs whereby it is in the HMO's financial best interest to provide minimal care to its patients. Tests a physician recommends can be *denied* by the HMO's utilization review committee. This committee may also *delay* the decision to the point that it is too late. Even worse, the physician can be reprimanded or fired for ordering too many tests or procedures, in spite of the fact that they are medically necessary.

HOW TO CHALLENGE AN HMO THAT DENIES YOU NECESSARY HEALTH CARE

Example: A patient admitted to a skilled nursing facility has had two weeks of physical therapy after a recent stroke. The HMO's case manager determines that this patient has become stable and—contrary to the recommendations of the HMO's physician and physician therapist—determines that the patient will not benefit from further physical therapy. This patient is entitled to rehabilitation for 60 days under traditional Medicare. But the case manager orders the patient to discontinue physical therapy and go to custodial care or be discharged to his home.

First Appeal Option—The Medical Group: The patient can appeal through the medical group to which he has been assigned and which hired the case manager. In all likelihood, the medical group will support the case manager's findings, and deny the request.

Second Appeal Option—The Health Plan: The patient can next appeal through the health plan, which would need to determine if the cancellation of the physician-recommended therapy was appropriate. If the health plan denies the request and upholds the medical group's decision, the patient has three remaining options:

- *Health Plan's Formal Appeal Process:* This process is usually self-serving for the health plan and a waste of the member's time once a decision has been made.

- *State Department of Insurance or Department of Corporations:* You may appeal the HMO's decision to the Department that oversees HMOs in your state.

- *Center for Health Dispute Resolution (CHDR):* This is the best of the three options. If you appeal to the CHDR and it decides in your favor, you can then have the HMO (1) provide the appropriate care and treatment or (2) pay for the care and treatment you obtained in the interim. If you obtain an unfavorable response from the CHDR, you can proceed to the Administrative Law Justice (ALJ) through Medicare Division of Social Security. At that time, you may wish to contact a lawyer to help with the presentation to the ALJ. If you believe your matter is urgent, let the health plan, the CHDR, and the ALJ know. Sometimes, a shorter waiting period will be provided to you.

CHAPTER 9

How ordinary people have fought HMOs ...and won!

In recent months, our law firm has taken on more than 10 new cases a week involving people who want to sue their insurance companies or HMOs for refusing to pay their medical claims. That's a big jump from over a year ago, when we saw only a couple of new cases a week.

The reason for the jump is that many more health insurance providers are coming up with a wider variety of ways to evade their legal responsibilities—and to reduce costs at the patients' expense.

Here are three cases my law firm recently settled involving patients who took on their health insurers—and won.

CASE #1: ENLISTING THE MEDIA

Three years ago, a health insurance company decided to halt coverage of specialized at-home care for a seven-year-old boy.

He was born with a rare heart and lung ailment that can cause dangerous health complications while he sleeps. As a result, he requires constant overnight monitoring at home by machines and a nurse.

By day, he is an honor student, plays baseball, and takes acting classes—none of which affects his condition.

The cost of his at-home care is nearly $150,000 a year. It had been covered by insurance ever since his illness was diagnosed when he was six weeks old.

But problems began when his father's employer switched medical plans. The new insurer determined that the at-home care was no longer medically necessary.

One month later, payment for the overnight care stopped. His mother appealed to the insurer, but the doctors who reviewed the case for the insurer maintained that the special care was not needed to keep the boy alive. That was when we filed a lawsuit against the father's health insurance company—and the company that reviewed medical claims for the insurance company.

The boy's mother wrote to local politicians and newspapers, and also went on national talk shows to tell her story. She was persistent and media savvy. Over and over, she told the story of her son and her complaints that the insurer had disregarded the recommendations of her son's personal doctor—a pediatric pulmonologist who had cared for him since birth.

Four months later, a court ordered the insurer to pay for the home health care until the lawsuit was settled. While preparing for trial, we found that the doctors retained by the new insurance company were unqualified to review a case as complicated as this one. None of them had expertise with pediatric heart and lung disease, and one of the doctors was a 73-year-old internist who had never even practiced pediatric medicine.

We also discovered that the contract with the insurer had a "savings clause" that created a financial incentive for doctors to deny treatment.

Result: The case was settled out of court—two-and-a-half years after we filed suit. Not only did the insurer agree to pay the cost of the boy's $150,000-a-year home nursing care for as long as he needs it, the company also paid more than $1 million in emotional distress damages to the mother and son.

Lesson: A major factor in our victory was the aggressive and indefatigable media campaign the mother waged on behalf of her son. She was tireless in talking about his predicament and used every opportunity to share their story with someone who might be able to help.

CASE #2: GAINING DOCTORS' SUPPORT

About two years ago, a 68-year-old man signed up with an HMO. Under the contract, he agreed to assign his Medicare benefits to the HMO in return for coverage to match or exceed minimum Medicare benefits. Among the promised benefits were 100% payment of comprehensive inpatient and outpatient rehabilitation services.

Six months after he enrolled in the HMO, the man broke his hip in a fall. After surgery, he suffered serious complications, including two major heart attacks, pneumonia, and a large blood clot in his leg. When he was finally moved out of the intensive care unit two months later, he was still unable to walk or stand.

The man needed extensive rehabilitation, so he was transferred by the hospital to a rehabilitation facility, where he began a physical therapy program.

But the HMO questioned whether the patient had the medical ability and stamina to participate in the program. Instead, the HMO mandated that he be admitted to a nursing home—which was less expensive but had no rehabilitation program.

His physicians maintained that, after physical therapy, the man could get back to work. Therefore, a nursing home was not appropriate. The HMO refused to pay for his inpatient and outpatient physical therapy on the grounds that it was not medically necessary.

We initiated legal action against the HMO as soon as it began to oppose his physical therapy. Fortunately, while waiting for the lawsuit to be settled, he was able to continue getting physical therapy with the help of a charitable foundation. He eventually made a full recovery.

Three years after filing suit, the patient received a multimillion-dollar settlement from the HMO.

Key to his victory: The unanimous support of all three of his doctors—his personal physician, his hospital physician, and his hospital psychiatrist. The physical therapy services they recommended were clearly within Medicare guidelines. But their decisions had been overruled by HMO representatives who were getting paid to say no.

CASE #3: LOOK FOR VIOLATIONS

A 61-year-old high school teacher was diagnosed with advanced breast cancer after being continuously covered by the same health insurance plan for more than 30 years.

Originally, she was insured under her husband's group policy at work, but later her own policy provided primary coverage and her husband's policy provided secondary coverage.

The double coverage meant that her husband's policy would cover part of whatever her policy did not.

Once her cancer was diagnosed, the woman underwent chemotherapy. Then her doctors determined that her only hope for a cure was to undergo a bone-marrow transplant.

When her physician sought authorization for the procedure, both her and her husband's insurance companies denied her coverage. They said the treatment was not medically necessary...that it was "experimental in nature," or that it was not proven to be effective.

Since time was running out, she had the bone-marrow transplant—despite the denial of her claim. Part of the more than $200,000 total cost was raised by donations. Fortunately, the transplant hospital agreed to accept her as a patient with a partial payment.

Result: After three years of legal wrangling, we settled the case for $1.5 million.

Lesson: Bone-marrow transplants are considered routine treatment for advanced breast cancer, not experimental in nature. The weight of medical opinion and court cases supports this treatment approach.

In addition, some years earlier, both the woman's policy and her husband's had been changed to reduce coverage for certain benefits, including bone-marrow transplants. But no notices of these reductions were ever provided to the woman or her husband. We argued that this was a violation of the law in her state.

Bottom line: Keep careful records, and never be afraid to fight back against your insurer. Your chances of success are always better if you can document your case, enlist your doctors' support, take your story to the media, and find alternative ways to pay the bills until your case can be heard.

CHAPTER 10

ANSWERS
TO THE 9 MOST
COMMONLY ASKED
COVERAGE
QUESTIONS

Millions of Americans have no problems with their health insurance. They file the necessary forms ...their claims are paid...and all parties are satisfied.

Problem: The higher the ultimate amount of your claim, the more likely you are to encounter a violation of your insurance contract by your insurer.

Due to the complexity of the laws governing insurance, what insurers can—and what they can't—do is often unclear. Here are some of the most common questions policyholders must face regarding their insurance coverage.

1. Can my insurer change or reduce my coverage?

Unfortunately, yes. *Key:* The insurer must give policy-holders early notice of the changes.

Recommended: Read all mail from your insurer—carefully. Often, such notices are buried in communications that appear to be junk mail.

Self-defense: If the reduction in coverage is made before you have a health problem, complain to your employer or union or switch policies.

2. What if the coverage is reduced after I have filed a claim?

It is unclear if insurers can legally reduce coverage once a policyholder is "on claim" for a particular accident or illness. Nevertheless, insurance companies have recently been getting away with it in court.

Reason: Every state has consumer protection rules that limit an insurer's ability to change coverage in midstream. But for individuals insured through their employers, state laws are preempted by the federal ERISA law.

Unfortunately, some courts are sympathetic to insurers rather than individual policyholders in the belief that premiums will rise if insurers are forced to pay all of the claims they have contracted to pay.

Example: Recently, a man who was insured under his employer's self-insurance plan had the $1 million AIDS coverage his policy promised reduced to a mere $5,000—after he became ill. Under ERISA, the court allowed the reduced benefit to stand.

In this controversial area, trial attorneys take the position that this is a vesting issue, that once a person is "on claim," it is illegal to reduce benefits.

Self-defense: Seek legal advice if your benefits are reduced after you are on claim.

3. Can I be dropped from a group, or can my health insurance be canceled?

Generally, no. If you are insured as a member of a group, the insurer would have to cancel the entire group. It is illegal to single out just one person.

Exception: If you are insured through your employer and become so seriously injured or ill that you cannot work, your insurer may try to claim that your employment relationship has ended. Thus, you are no longer part of the group—and can be canceled in mid-claim.

Again, this is a gray area. Many states prohibit this type of cancellation, but the state laws are negated under ERISA. Trial attorneys say that a person is vested if he/she becomes injured or ill while employed. Case law precedent holds that the insurer must continue to cover claims resulting from that particular illness or injury. But, some courts have held otherwise.

Self-defense: Check your insurance contract for conditions under which you can be dropped. They are usually headed "Termination of Coverage." Don't automatically accept a cancellation if it occurs. This area of law is technical and esoteric. Seek an attorney who is experienced in this area.

There are cases in which an insurer has dropped an entire group of policyholders, claiming it's discontinuing its group health coverage business. State laws that once required insurers to provide alternate coverage for such policyholders have been negated under ERISA, leaving large numbers of people uninsured, and uninsurable, in mid-claim.

4. When can my insurer decide that my new claim was a pre-existing condition?

This is an area where policyholders frequently fail to get the coverage they believe they are paying for. Carefully check your policy for conditions that are excluded for either a certain amount of time or altogether.

General rule: For an insurer to deem a condition "pre-existing," you must have seen a doctor for the condition, and had a symptom the doctor could diagnose as indicating that condition, before your insurance policy taking effect.

Everyone may have the symptomless beginnings of an undetected health problem. But some insurers stretch their definition of "pre-existing."

Example: A man is denied coverage for his heart attack because his doctor told him he had high cholesterol three years earlier and recommended that he watch his diet.

Self-defense: Challenge the denial. Your condition must have been diagnosable to be considered pre-existing. If it wasn't diagnosed, you have a strong case for coverage. Even if it *was* diagnosed, you may be able to prove is wasn't pre-existing.

5. Can insurers apply exclusions in an unfair way?

They can, and they do. Coverage exclusions are legal,

and common for entire categories of treatment, such as alcoholism, drug dependence, and psychiatric care.

Caution: Insurers may try to "weasel out" of coverage related to these exclusions. *Example:* An insurer may deny coverage for a liver ailment, claiming it was a result of alcoholism and is therefore excluded.

Self-defense: Challenge the denial. It's the liver that is being treated, not the alcoholism.

Insurers also tend to deny coverage based on broad interpretation of legitimate exclusions.

Examples: Experimental treatment...medical versus "custodial" care...treatment or hospital days that are "not medically necessary."

Danger area: Policies that pay for accidents but not illnesses. *Catch:* You file a claim for injuries resulting from a fall. The insurer says the fall was caused by dizziness resulting from a disease, so the fall was not accidental.

6. Can the opinion of an insurance company's doctor overrule my doctor's judgment?

Usually, yes. A number of insurance policies even state that the insurer reserves the right to have its own "medical director" make a final determination when benefits are being disputed.

Problem: As an employee of the insurer, this medical director almost always rules against the policyholder.

Self-defense: The best insurance contracts state that the deciding opinion in a claim will be by the policyholder's treating physician.

Reality: Most insurers will not put this issue in writing, and most insurance policies say nothing about who decides in the event of a dispute.

Exception: A union or large corporation may be able to negotiate an appropriate clause in its contract.

7. What if there is a disagreement on what is considered a "reasonable and customary charge" for a certain medical procedure?

Often, a portion of a medical claim will be denied on the basis that the policy only covers set "customary charges."

Reason: Insurance companies often base these rates on old schedules or national averages that don't take regional differences into account. Most people don't contest the "small stuff." And adjusters know it.

Self-defense: Survey health providers in your area, and document customary charges for your procedure. Ask the claims handler what "relative value scale" or "code" was used to measure reasonable and customary charges. In the face of evidence, insurers usually back down.

Threat: A class action suit based on your research could cost them millions.

8. What if my pre-authorized medical procedure is denied?

Pre-approval of medical treatment does not guarantee an airtight claim. Many current lawsuits concern the denial of claims after the treatments were pre-certified by the insurance company.

Examples: Hospitalizations the adjuster calls "custodial" rather than treatment-related, and heart transplants or bone-marrow transplants for cancer patients, often costing $100,000 and up, that are determined to be experimental—after they were approved.

Trap: Often, a clerk will pre-certify a general medical procedure or course of treatment, which an adjuster will later withdraw.

Self-defense: Have your doctor write in for general pre-certification of any serious procedure. Have it done, and fight later if you have to.

9. What can I do to protect myself?

It's impossible to be totally secure, no matter what your insurance contract says. But there are ways to minimize risk. *Suggestions:*

- If your employer offers a choice of insurers, investigate the claims records of each company. Inquire about each insurer's history of paying claims, delays versus timeliness, invoking exclusions and pre-existing conditions, etc.
- To have more clout when contesting a claim, consider buying additional group insurance that is not provided through an employer and thus does not fall under the jurisdiction of ERISA. Such policies are regulated by state insurance law and therefore allow for easier recourse if problems arise.

Examples: Plans offered through professional associations, organizations such as AARP, NOW, and many others.

CHAPTER 11

THE AWFUL ERISA SCANDAL—HOW A LAW MEANT TO PROTECT YOU IS HURTING YOU

Did you know that if you and your family are insured through your employer, you have no legal recourse if your insurance company unfairly delays or denies your medical claim, or cancels your insurance coverage altogether, and as a result, you suffer damaging consequences? You cannot sue your HMO if your health is further impaired when a costly treatment is delayed or denied...or your credit is damaged when your medical bills go unpaid...or you liquidate your savings, retirement account, or other interest earnings funds when you must pay medical bills yourself...or you are forced to declare bankruptcy...or your home is foreclosed on as the result of unbearable debt...or you suffer mental distress from any of the above. Unbelievable as it sounds, your only recourse against your managed care company is to go to court to recover the cost of the treatment it should have given you in the first place.

Though far from the original intent of the law, a loophole in the Employee Retirement Income Security Act (ERISA) gives insurance companies immunity from damage suits.

THE BACKGROUND

ERISA, a federal law created to protect all employee-welfare benefit plans—retirement, pension, group health insurance, etc.—was passed in 1974. The law was clearly intended to improve employees' rights. Enforcement of the law falls under the jurisdiction of the Department of Labor, which is supposed to serve as a watchdog and investigate complaints filed under ERISA provisions.

Problems: The Labor Department has had no history of expertise in the area of health insurance, which traditionally has been regulated on the state level by 50 state departments of insurance. But employer-sponsored group health insurance plans have become increasingly prevalent.

- *Covered by ERISA:* 85% of Americans who have group health insurance benefits through their employers, including small businesses.

- *Not covered by ERISA:* School employees, individuals who work for the government, people who are insured through a church, individuals on Medicare and Medicaid, and those who are privately insured.

ERISA can be tricky, so it's a good idea to consult an attorney if you think you fall into a gray area.

From 1974 to 1987, people whose benefits were covered by ERISA, and who had a dispute with their insurance company, were able to sue for compensation according to the consumer protection laws in their state. But in 1987, a Supreme Court decision (*Pilot Life v. Dedeaux*) held that state consumer laws are preempted—indeed, superseded—by ERISA.

Negative consequences: ERISA is now the group policyholders' only tool to fight back when they are cheated by an insurance company. But when it comes to health insurance, ERISA has no teeth. Employees are no longer permitted to...

- Sue their health insurer for consequential, compensatory, or punitive damages arising from unfair or even fraudulent claims denials.
- Recover damages for loss of health, life, property, income, or peace of mind.

Insurance companies are liable only for the amount of benefits that were improperly denied, and, at the discretion of the judge, attorneys' fees.

Result: An explosion of bad faith practices by insurance companies, particularly in cases of catastrophic illness or injury. The powerful HMO industry enjoys no accountability and no liability. Consumers, meanwhile, have no remedy in the courts and no way to penalize HMOs for the way they do business. And without the threat of a potential lawsuit, managed care companies may have no incentive to make the right medical decisions on behalf of their patients.

EFFECT ON THE TAXPAYER

Insurance companies know they can deny claims without any accountability, even when they do so intentionally or negligently. The present law protects insurance carriers by making them immune from any damages (emotional distress, loss of life) except the specific benefits originally owed.

The practice of denying coverage for long-term progressive diseases, such as terminal cancer, long-term disability and AIDS, is becoming widespread. The burden of paying for this catastrophic care is systematically being shifted to the taxpayer. Furthermore, someone whose benefits have been unfairly denied and must seek public assistance has no incentive to recover those benefits on behalf of the state or Medicare.

SETTLING DISPUTES

Prior to 1987, over 90% of insurance disputes were settled outside the courtroom, often through mediation by the consumer affairs divisions of the various state departments of insurance. The remaining cases were often taken on by attorneys who were willing to work on a contingency basis.

Since 1987, few policyholders or attorneys can afford to bring suit in an ERISA insurance case because so little money can be recovered.

The Department of Labor has no administrative staff, procedures, or jurisdiction to settle claims. It receives more than 10,000 complaints each year from consumers who feel they have been unfairly denied medical benefits. If the Department of Labor were to establish procedures for negotiating these claims, it would do so at further expense to the taxpayer.

WHAT YOU CAN DO

Write, telegram, or fax your federal representatives, insisting that they pass legislation that would close the ERISA loophole and would restore states' rights to enforce insurance laws. (See page 89 for a Sample Letter to Your Member of Congress.)

If you know of people who are suffering as a result of unfair denials, delays, or cancellation of group insurance benefits, encourage them to contact their federal representatives and members of the House Committee on Education and Labor, Subcommittee on Labor-Management Relations, and the US Senate Committee on Labor.

If you are responsible for administering company benefits plans, do not be taken in by insurance company lobbyists who claim that allowing victims of unfair insurance company practices to collect damages will increase the cost of health insurance to employers.

Ironic: The cost of health insurance to employers has risen over 5% faster since the key 1987 court decision, than it did in the 13 years under ERISA previous to the decision—when lawsuits for punitive and compensatory damages were allowed!

Every citizen and corporation in this country is responsible for the payment of damages and can be criminally prosecuted if they are found guilty of fraud...except for insurance companies enjoying the ERISA loophole. As consumers, we don't have to accept this!

CASE HISTORY

CANCER PATIENT DIES FROM HMO DELAYS, HAS NO REMEDY

PHYLLIS CANNON
Oklahoma City, OK
R.I.P.

Phyllis Cannon's health insurer delayed her medically appropriate cancer treatment for three months. By that time her cancer had developed beyond treatment, and she died weeks later.

In 1991, Phyllis Cannon was diagnosed with acute myeloblastic leukemia. When she went into remission, her doctor urged that she undergo an autologous bone-marrow transplant (ABMT). But her HMO delayed authorization for three months. By that time it was too late. The cancer had returned and Mrs. Cannon could no longer benefit from the treatment.

Cannon's HMO claimed that transplants would be "experimental," even though this procedure was a covered benefit under Cannon's policy. She died just a few weeks later.

Because Mrs. Cannon received health insurance through her employer, the ERISA loophole prevented her family from recovering damages from the HMO for its delay of treatment and gave her husband, Jerry Cannon, no remedy for his wife's death.

Judge John Porfilio, of the Tenth Circuit Court of Appeal, noted the problem of ERISA's broad preemption of remedies for wrongful death, stating that "Although moved by the tragic circumstances of this case, and the seemingly needless loss of life that resulted, we conclude that the law gives us no choice but to affirm" that Mr. Cannon has no remedy for his loss.

ERISA Casualty of the Day, June 22, 1998

Consumers for
Quality ✚ Care

CASE HISTORY

HMO REFUSES REFERRALS TO SPECIALISTS AND PATIENT LOSES HIS LEGS

MISAC NEGOSIAN
Sunland, CA

On February 1993, Misac Negosian suffered an arteriosclerotic aneurysm, or stroke, leaving him with a limp in his left leg. Misac requested a referral to a cardiologist, neurologist, and cardiovascular disease specialist, but his HMO primary care physician instead called the stroke an "accident" caused by the stress of Negosian's unemployment.

In May 1996, Misac suffered a major blood clot in his left leg and had to go to the hospital. The HMO refused to pay for the ambulance transport, so Misac had to use a private service. After three hours at the HMO hospital, Misac's skyrocketing blood pressure forced the HMO to allow him to see one of its cardiovascular surgeons. The HMO surgeon attempted a bypass surgery, but extensive damage had already been done. A week later, Misac's left leg was amputated above the knee.

A few days after the amputation, the HMO sent Misac to a convalescent hospital, but refused to pay for ambulance transport to his frequent medical appointments at the HMO. Four months later, with his condition getting worse, Misac had to have his right leg amputated below the knee.

Misac's medical records show that in 1986 he was diagnosed with the genetic condition homocystinuria, which was discovered in the early 1990's to be linked with arteriovascular disease and renal failure. However, Misac had continually been told his problems were all due to kidney failure. He even had surgery in 1991 to have fibrosis removed from his kidneys.

If Misac's HMO had properly treated his stroke in 1993, it would have discovered the link between homocystinuria and renal failure, and Misac's legs probably could have been saved. Instead, Misac did not receive proper treatment until after 1996 when the severity of the disease necessitated amputation.

Misac Negosian had the ability to walk taken from him. Because Misac receives his healthcare through his wife's employer, his HMO can claim immunity from damages under a loophole in the federal ERISA law.

ERISA Casualty of the Day, July 16, 1990

Consumers for Quality ✚ Care

CASE HISTORY

AT-RISK MOTHER NOT ADMITTED TO HOSPITAL...LOSES BABY, HAS NO REMEDY

FLORENCE CORCORAN
Slidell, LA

Florence Corcoran's tragic case has become the most frequently cited precedent used by HMOs hiding from state lawsuits.

Corcoran was faced with a high-risk pregnancy. Her obstetrician ordered her hospitalized. Her HMO overruled her doctor and denied the hospitalization, even though Corcoran had a second opinion agreeing with the doctor's advice. Instead, Corcoran's insurer ordered home nursing care for only 10 hours each day.

During the last month of Corcoran's pregnancy, when no nurse was on duty, the baby went into distress. Without the monitors and care of a hospital, the baby died.

Because Corcoran received her health insurance through her employer, the ERISA loophole freed her insurer from liability. Mrs. Corcoran's wrongful death action in Louisiana state court, alleging medical malpractice, was preempted.

Fifth Circuit Court of Appeal Judge Carolyn Dineen King ruled in the case that "the basic facts are undisputed," but "the result ERISA compels us to reach means that the Corcorans have no remedy, state, or federal, for what may have been a serious mistake." She continued, saying ERISA "eliminates an important check on the thousands of medical decisions routinely made. With liability rules generally inapplicable, there is theoretically less deterrence of substandard medical making."

"If I go out on the street and murder a person, I am thrown in jail for murder and held accountable," said Corcoran. "What's the difference between me and this clerk thousands of

miles away making a life decision which took the life of my baby, and she gets off scot-free and keeps her job? Insurance companies don't answer to anybody. Nobody knows about ERISA."

ERISA Casualty of the Day, May 11, 1998

Consumers for Quality ✚ Care

CASE HISTORY

HMO DENIES QUADRIPLEGIC CHILD VITAL THERAPY AND CHANCE TO WALK

ETHAN BEDRICK
Raleigh, NC

Ethan Bedrick was born January 28, 1992. During the delivery, there were complications and he lost oxygen. As a result, he suffers from severe cerebral palsy and spastic quadriplegia. Hypertonia from the quadriplegia impairs the motor functions in all four of his limbs.

Without proper treatment, Ethan can get much worse. His muscles must be stretched regularly to avoid shortening and inflexibility. Therefore, he was put on an intense regimen of physical, occupational and speech therapy to assist him throughout his development.

When Ethan was 14 months old, his HMO unexpectedly cut off coverage of his speech therapy and limited his physical and occupational therapy to only 15 sessions per year. This recommendation was made by an HMO doctor who had never even personally met Ethan! The reviewing HMO doctor performed a "utilization review" of Ethan's case to look for ways to cut off or reduce unnecessary services. She then called Ethan's pediatrician who told her that Ethan had a 50% chance to walk by the age of 5. The reviewing HMO doctor decided this prognosis was of "minimal benefit" for further therapy, and so Ethan's coverage was cut.

Ethan's coverage was reviewed again in October 1993. Again, it was denied. The second HMO doctor further denied Ethan prescribed therapeutic equipment, including a bath chair and an upright walker. It claimed they were merely "convenience items," not to be covered by the HMO.

In 1994, exhausted and out of options, the Bedricks

filed suit in state court against the HMO. The HMO had the suit removed to federal court where it would be shielded by the federal ERISA law.

The federal circuit court concluded in 1996 that the HMO's decision to restrict Ethan's therapy was "arbitrary and capricious," and their doctors' opinions were found to be groundless and riddled with conflict. The court also ruled that the HMO's guidelines do not require "significant progress" as a precondition to providing medically necessary treatments.

The court further stated, "it is as important not to get worse as it is to get better. The implication that walking by age five...would not be 'significant progress' for this unfortunate child is simply revolting."

Still, because of ERISA, the Bedricks are left with no means for restitution for Ethan's therapy loss, and face the future with only limited care and equipment for him. The HMO will pay no damages.

ERISA Casualty of the Day, June 29, 1998

Consumers for Quality ✚ Care

SAMPLE LETTER TO YOUR MEMBER OF CONGRESS

[DATE]

The Honorable [Full Name of Senator]	The Honorable [Full Name of Representative]
United States Senate	United States House of Representatives
Washington, D.C. 20510	Washington, D.C. 20515

OR

Dear [Full Name of Senator/Representative]:

I urge you to support legislation making HMOs accountable to the people they serve.

Employees who receive health care benefits from a private sector employer have little or no remedy when their claim is wrongfully denied. Under ERISA, state laws providing damages against wrongdoers are unavailable and HMOs are responsible for only the cost of the care they should have provided in the first place.

I urge you to pass legislation that would:

• Close the ERISA loophole that allows HMOs to escape liability. HMO patients with employer-paid health care should have the same right to sue that every other citizen enjoys.

• We want *doctors*—not managed care bureaucrats—to make important medical decisions. Don't let managed care companies get away with practicing bad medicine.

I know there are many bills pending. Please support legislation that makes HMOs liable in court. That is the only way they will ever be held accountable to their patients.

Sincerely,

[Your Full Name and Address]

CHAPTER 12

What to do if an insurance company tries to rescind your policy

I n their efforts to cut costs, insurance companies are increasingly likely to cancel your policy when you file a claim—rather than pay out—especially if the coverage is for a large sum.

This practice by insurance companies, known as rescission, has become a major problem for consumers, particularly in the areas of health, life, disability, and malpractice insurance. Although the insurer who cancels under those circumstances must refund the premiums paid over the lifetime of the policy, the consumer is left without insurance and will find that it's harder to get a new policy.

HOW RESCISSION WORKS

Although a policy is a contract, an insurance company can legally cancel the policy if it finds that a policyholder lied or failed to disclose pertinent information before the agreement was signed.

That can include nondisclosure of a driving violation on an auto-insurance policy, a medical condition on a health, life, or disability policy, or pending litigation on a malpractice insurance policy.

Insurers are supposed to "underwrite" or investigate policies at the time of the application to determine if the consumer is qualified. But in practice, most insurers approve policies and accept policyholder premiums—and then check medical and other records only when a claim is filed. This practice is called "post-claims underwriting."

Once the claim is on file, the insurer is more likely to go back and look for any flaw in the original application and contract so it can cancel the policy. It can search at any time through confidential materials such as computerized data and various medical records. The policyholder granted the insurer permission to do this when he/she signed the application.

Trap: By studying these records, an insurer may learn about conditions or medical treatment that you disclosed to your doctors or lawyers but did not mention on your insurance policy application.

REDUCING THE ODDS

- *Self-defense:* Don't misrepresent facts on insurance applications. If you smoke, for example, don't claim you're a nonsmoker in order to qualify for a lower premium. An insurance company can rescind your life or health insurance policy even if the reason you're filing a claim has nothing to do with smoking.

- *Self-defense:* Make sure your agent writes down your answers. In the event of an oversight or dispute, agents often side with the insurer. Telling the insurance company, "I told the agent when we met that I had high blood pressure" is not a strong defense, since it will only pit your word against the agent's.

- *Self-defense:* Beware of vague questions. Some insurance applications purposefully ask broad questions or use open-ended words to provide insurers with loopholes in the future, or both.

Examples: "Have you ever had...?" "List all doctors you have ever seen, and what for..." *Solution:* Ask your agent to be specific by asking him/her such questions as, "What does the insurer mean by a 'back disorder?'"

- *Self-defense:* Read your application before sign-ing it. This is especially important if an agent has read you the questions. Insurance applications can be very detailed. In addition, agents fre-quently read questions fast, paraphrase or simply check off boxes.

- *Self-defense:* If you have group coverage through your employer, make sure you are actually eligible. Many employers withhold or collect premiums for medical insurance from part-time employees. But employees who work less than 20-30 hours a week are often ineligible for group coverage. As a result, your company's insurer may cancel your policy when you file a claim, especially if it's a large one.

- *Self-defense:* Consider going back to clean up your application. Since you would be correcting your application and not filing a claim, it is like-ly that the insurer would just take down the information. *Caution:* If you failed to disclose a significant condition, such as a chronic back problem, your insurer may send you a rider excluding coverage for the problem.

FIGHTING BACK

If your policy is canceled and you believe the grounds for the rescission are baseless, fight to keep your insurance. *Here's what you can do:*

- **Know your rights.** Courts nationwide have ruled that insurers cannot use trivial or immaterial nondisclosures to rescind policies. There are no grounds for rescission if...
- The insurer would have issued the insurance policy even if the condition were disclosed.
- The applicant had no present knowledge of a condition or failed to appreciate the significance of an incorrect or incomplete response.

Example: Several years before applying for life insurance, a man was told that his blood pressure was running a little high, but his doctor didn't prescribe any treatment. Because he wasn't treated for the problem at the time, his insurer would not be able to rescind the policy based on this nondisclosure, even if the man later died of a heart attack.

Example: A young, divorced, working mother in California who filed a claim for breast-cancer treatment was told that her policy was being rescinded because she had failed to disclose that she had a "nervous disease or disorder." The insurance company discovered that, several years earlier, she and her ex-husband had visited a psychologist for marital counseling.

The court found that the insurer had acted in bad faith by contriving a groundless rescission and awarded the woman's medical bills paid, plus $500,000 in damages.

- **Write to the insurance company immediately, contesting the rescission.** Explain why you believe any alleged nondisclosure was insignificant or overlooked. Often, resistance on the part of the policyholder is all that is required for an insurer to reverse its decision.

- **If necessary, enlist the help of your state's Department of Insurance.** Keep in mind, however, that this can be a lengthy process and you may be without insurance until the matter is resolved.

If all else fails, contact a trial attorney with experience in insurance matters. Be sure to keep all records and materials relating to the policy, both before and after you signed the document. Also keep all correspondence between you and the insurer.

WHEN YOU CAN RESCIND YOUR INSURANCE POLICY

Rescission cuts both ways. You can, in fact, cancel your policy and have your premiums refunded. Here are situations in which this might be wise...

- The insurance company, agent, or its advertising can be shown to have misrepresented or omitted promised coverage.
- The insurance company or agent failed to disclose material information that would have caused the policyholder not to purchase the policy.
- The contract turns out to be illegal...or the policyholder is ineligible.

Example: Someone who purchases a second disability policy may find out that it overlaps the original policy and exceeds the disability carriers' participation limits. If the insurer is aware of this, the policy should not have been issued.

Example: A nurse who was having an affair with a married doctor took out a life insurance policy on him. To keep the policy out of his taxable estate, they decided she would call herself a "business associate." *Problem*: The woman later found out that, according to law, she did not have an "insurable interest" in the doctor, since she was neither his spouse nor his business partner. The contract was illegal, so she rescinded the policy, and the insurance company was required to return her premiums.

CHAPTER 13

How to Challenge an Insurance Company That Refuses Your Legitimate Claim

About 10% of all insurance claims are unjustly denied. But fewer than 1% of people making insurance claims even question their insurer when their claim is refused.

Insurance companies routinely maximize their profits based on the expectation that policyholders will passively accept their decisions.

Result: Millions of small, honest claims are denied and never challenged.

Important: The majority of policyholders who do contest denied claims either win their cases or improve their settlements.

Steps to take when faced with an insurance ruling you believe to be unfair...

- **Don't assume that the first "no" you receive is final.** Insurers often change their rulings when challenged.

- **Insist on a written explanation.** Most state laws require insurance companies to provide written explanations of claim denials. Failure to comply may constitute an illegal practice by the insurer.

- **Read your policy carefully to determine if the claim was legitimately denied.** The insurance company may have interpreted a clause in your policy differently from the way you understand it. Respect your own sense of fairness and what you expected the policy to cover. If the ruling doesn't sound fair, there's a good chance that it isn't.

The language in an insurance policy will be interpreted as a lay person would understand it. Courts have concluded that *policy provisions will be interpreted based on the reasonable expectations of the policyholder, not the insurer.*

- **Do not accept filing errors as grounds for refusal.** Always follow your insurer's instructions for filing a claim. But if you fail to fill out a form correctly, or if you miss a deadline for submitting a claim—even if you are months late—an insurance company cannot refuse to pay an otherwise valid claim unless the company can show it has been harmed by your error or prevented from making an adequate investigation due to the delay.

- **Do your own research to support your claim.** A woman's insurance company paid $500 less than she expected toward the cost of her emergency Caesarean section, stating that her physician charged beyond what was "reasonable and customary." She called every OB/GYN in her area, and found that only three charged less than her own doctor, while most charged the same and ten charged more. *Result:* The insurer had to agree that the fee was "reasonable and customary" for her area, and it paid the bill.

- **Ask your insurance agent or group policy administrator at work for support.** The agent from whom you purchased your insurance has a duty to make sure the coverage protects your interests.

If you have group medical coverage with your employer, the company may have an administrator who will intervene with the insurer on your behalf. A nudge from one of these intermediaries is often all it takes for an insurance company to settle a policyholder's complaint.

- **Contact the insurance company directly.** If your insurance agent or claims administrator doesn't resolve the problem within 30 days, telephone the insurance company yourself. Be polite but persistent, and keep going up the corporate ladder. Be sure to make a record of all phone calls, including the names and positions of everyone with whom you speak. Save your phone bills that list the calls.

Follow up each call with a brief letter stating your understanding of the conversations, and requesting a response within 30 days. Willingness to be a "squeaky wheel" is often all that is required to resolve minor disputes, misunderstandings, errors, or unintentional claims mishandlings.

- **Complain in writing if your phone calls don't work.** Begin with the person who denied your claim, then write to that person's supervisor. Include your policy number, copies of all relevant forms, bills, and supporting documents and a clear, concise description of the problem. Request that the insurer responds in writing within three weeks. Keep copies of all correspondence. Send letters by registered mail. Explain what negative effects the denial of your claim is having.

Key: A courteous, unemotional tone. Avoid rude or blaming statements.

Surprising: Insurance companies often pay claims once they hear the policyholder's side of the story. Or they may offer an acceptable compromise or explain the denial in a way you find satisfactory.

Keep in mind that HMOs and other health insurers are very sensitive to negative publicity, especially in the current anti-HMO climate. While it's never a good idea to threaten your insurer, you can use the media to your advantage. If you're involved in a high-profile case, you might want to consider alerting the media on your own.

- **Write a follow-up letter.** If you receive no response, send follow-up letters, with your original letter attached to the insurance company's consumer complaints or customer service department and to the company president. *Helpful:* In most states, failure to respond promptly to letters regarding claims is an unfair insurance practice.

- **Enlist outside help.** If necessary, add pressure from...

  - Your state Department of Insurance. *Cost:* Free. The amount these departments can help consumers varies from state to state. But some states with strong departments (California, New York, Illinois) will mediate your dispute.

  - A professional arbitrator. *Cost:* Your time plus filing fees (usually low).

  - A lawyer. *Cost:* On a contingency basis so that you'll be charged only if you win your case. If you already have an attorney on retainer, a letter from his/her office may do the trick.

CHAPTER 14

USING THE LAW OF INSURANCE BAD FAITH TO FIGHT BACK

Insurance companies insist they sell protection. But, as soon as a policyholder files a claim, an adversarial attitude sets in. The attitude is that a policyholder is wrong and the insurance company is right. Then the carrier can use endless technicalities, exclusions, and ambiguities to say "Claim Denied."

Many policyholders settle a claim for less than is due them. Rather than being rescued by the heroic images used by insurance companies such as Paul Revere, John Hancock, or Thomas Jefferson, the policyholder becomes victimized by accusations. He or she is charged with dishonesty, malingering, fraud, or even the act of committing arson. Understandably, the policyholder suddenly perceives his insurer as the enemy. An individual may have lost his health, house, and even family members—and now he faces the loss of self-respect as he defends himself against the charges of his insurance company.

Isn't it ironic that when we hear about insurance cheats, the first image that comes to mind is the guy who falsifies a claim in order to reap a bonanza from his insurance company? The industry public-relations mill creates a phantom American policyholder who stages an auto accident, burns down his house, injures himself to avoid work, or in extreme cases, even kills off relatives to collect death benefits.

Of course there is consumer fraud. When it occurs, all consumers suffer—in the pocketbook and in the distrust created of the system. An insurance carrier should not have to pay false claims. Insurance agents need time to investigate thoroughly and make a sound and fair decision. But to what extent is consumer fraud—as opposed to insurance fraud—occurring? Are both treated with equal weight under the law?

If a policyholder inflates property or auto damages, sets his car on fire, or commits arson, he is breaking the law and should be punished. Often a district attorney enters the case and the consumer can end up in jail. But how many insurance adjusters do you know who have been indicted for fraud? White-collar insurance executives—caught in well-documented corporate crimes against policyholders—do not end up in jail.

Meanwhile, the honest policyholders—who represent the large majority of consumers—are isolated and vulnerable when confronted with problems collecting legitimate benefits. Who is taking up their cause? Thousands of policyholders write letters of complaint to insurance companies that go largely unanswered. The responses they do give are usually double-talk, with meaningless standard insurance jargon. Occasionally, letters to state insurance departments may inspire a government bureaucrat to settle a dispute. In most cases, these bureaucrats are ineffective representatives of the consumer.

The law of bad faith is simple. If a policyholder's legitimate claim has been unreasonably denied, he can sue for more than the amount of his benefits. He can collect damages for his mental suffering and all economic loss caused by the company's refusal to honor his legitimate claim. If the insurance company's conduct demonstrates a conscious disregard for the rights of the policyholder, then the policyholder can sue for and recover punitive damages. The purpose of punitive damages is to punish and make examples out of companies that engage in outrageous behavior. A jury sets the amount of punitive damages based on the amount of money it will take to make an errant company change and start behaving more responsibly. The larger the company, the greater the amount of punitive damages. A $50 claim may now result in a multimillion-dollar judgment. (See actual case study in Chapter 15.)

In my law practice, I hear insurance horror stories every day. I hear of families hounded by collection agencies to pay medical bills that insurance companies should have paid in the first place. I hear of disabled people who are forced to go on welfare instead of collecting disability benefits due them under their insurance policies. In one case, a rental company repossessed a policyholder's wheelchair because the insurance carrier failed to make payments on her behalf. One woman became so distraught because the company would not pay her medical bills that she attempted suicide. Some businesses, large and small, have gone bankrupt when reluctant insurance companies refused to make timely payments.

CHAPTER 15

AN ACTUAL CASE STUDY

SENIOR CITIZEN TAKES HIS $48 HEALTH INSURANCE CLAIM TO COURT AND WINS BIG

Emotional Moment: Elmer Norman, 72, of Azusa, talks to reporters about his $4.5 million victory against a health insurer who denied a $48 claim. (AP Photo)

Elmer Norman was 72 when he walked into my office wearing a homemade hearing aid. He was almost deaf, and also blind in one eye. The slender elderly man had made his hearing aid by connecting stereo headphones to a box hooked to his belt. To ask questions, I had to speak through a microphone plugged into Elmer's device. He was a most unforgettable character with a $48 gripe.

Elmer told me how his health insurance company took advantage of him by refusing to pay a $48 claim. The company had refused to pay for his medicine and a hearing test. Insurance claims adjusters argued that the policy excluded the test as well as Elmer's prescription for medicine.

I joined Elmer in his $48 battle against the large insurance company. I never dreamed, though, that Elmer's case would become one of the greatest David and Goliath battles of my career.

Court congestion in California often results in months—sometimes years—of waiting before a trial can be set. Sometimes new facts emerge, and often memories fade. As the trial date neared, the insurance company attorneys wanted an updated deposition. They hoped to reassure themselves that they had missed nothing. The deposition gave them more than they bargained for.

In the deposition, Elmer rambled on, telling how his prospects for medical security had vanished and describing his various frustrations. Suddenly he forgot about his $48 claim and launched into a tirade about his benefits being reduced by a switch in policies. This was news to us and startled everyone. *Elmer explained:*

"I discovered to my horror and sorrow that...the insurance company was promising the sun, moon, and stars concerning improved benefits...but that what they promised as being improvements were really reductions in benefits. There was an increased deductible, new limitations on drugs...and a fantastic reduction for 80 percent of the allowable benefits in a certain number of categories down to only 20 percent."

Elmer's deposition made it clear that I needed to broaden his lawsuit to include the switch in policies. I amended the original documents to incorporate the charge that the insurance company had changed the policies fraudulently. That issue became the centerpiece of the lawsuit.

I filed the amended complaint, and new discovery proceedings began. I requested copies of all documents relevant to the policy switch. These revealed that the company's true intention was to revise the out-of-hospital coverage in order to reduce benefits by 40 percent. The policy switch would save the company over $4 million in payouts per year. Interoffice memos and directives detailed revisions that would make the new plan "appear similar" to the old plan. One memo stated:

"We are attempting to reduce claim payments by 40 percent...We propose two basic changes which...involve reducing the amount paid on medical supplies, X-rays, and laboratory tests [which are paid under Medicare] to 20 percent of eligible expenses and establishing a separate drug deductible."

Two other documents were equally damaging. These undated and unsigned memos, one handwritten, explained why the company was doing what it was doing and what the objectives were.

The second of these two, a typewritten list of objectives, summarized things nicely:

OBJECTIVES OF REVISION

1. *Reduce claims cost by 40 percent* [emphasis added].
2. Permit elimination of pre-existing condition exclusion.
3. Limit future claim cost inflation.
4. Prevent drug benefit dominance.
5. Minimize variety in coinsurance amounts.
6. *Appear similar to current plan* [emphasis added].

My enthusiasm for the case increased. I now had evidence that the insurance company switched policies on Elmer, and on thousands of other senior citizens like Elmer, telling them that this was a new and improved policy when actually the coverage was being reduced by 40 percent. We had the evidence of this scheme right from the insurance companies' own records. I was very anxious to bring this story in front of a jury because I felt strongly that this was a case where a jury would want to punish this insurance company for its "bad faith" behavior that affected many senior citizens who had been victims of the "switch." After all, it appeared to me they were making about a $4 million illicit profit a year by duping senior citizens.

The trial lasted 14 days and produced 1,331 pages of transcript.

One of the most interesting aspects of the trial was a letter that was sent to Elmer by the insurance company, informing him that his new policy contained "substantial improvements" in coverage. I kept coming back to the fact that I couldn't see any "improvements." There were some added areas of coverage in the new policy, but they involved medical costs arising from pregnancy or injury due to accidents while in the military.

I didn't for a second believe they would try to sell the idea to the jury that adding coverage for pregnancy or accidents while in the military would do anything for these senior citizens. But the insurance company's lawyer put on a straight face and tried to defend these additions by arguing to the jury that nothing prevented an older man from having a wife of childbearing age. The absurdity of awarding retired people maternity benefits was not lost on the jurors. Some laughed out loud.

This was all we needed to convince a jury that punishment was in order for this insurance company. Instead of apologizing to Elmer and to other senior citizens for attempting to hoodwink them out of 40 percent of their benefits, the company instead tried to justify its action by pointing to "benefits" in the new policy that were not really benefits at all.

During my closing argument I explained the value of punitive damage awards and the several ways these awards can be viewed. I asked the jury if it was punishment at all just to take back the money, the ill-gotten profits that the company had wrongfully made by this scheme. There was $4 million a year, and two years had already passed.

I told the jury that what this insurance company understood best was money. "Let's send them a legal message that has a dollar sign on it and tell them, 'This isn't the way you treat elderly people. If you're going to sell insurance to old people and you're going to make millions and millions of dollars, year after year, you better be fair to them. Because if you're not fair and you start to cut corners, and you commit fraud, an American jury may punish you.'"

I ended my closing argument to the jury by explaining that the purpose of the punitive damage award is not to compensate Elmer, but to deter the insurance company from engaging in fraudulent conduct in the future. I also told the jury that the insurance company should not be able to keep the money that it made by virtue of this fraudulent scheme. It had already made over $8 million by this "switch" in policies that duped many senior citizens out of their rightful benefits. I emphasized to the jury that it was extremely important that this company realize that this was not the way to do business. That in order for their verdict to be meaningful and to stop this type of practice in the future, the jurors were going to have to get the attention of management of the insurance company by a significant award.

Elmer, who had attended most sessions of the trial, stayed away during jury deliberations. I told him we would call him when the verdict came in. Two days later I was called by the Court Clerk informing me that there was a verdict. I called Elmer just before I left for the courthouse. Elmer's car broke down twice on the way to the courthouse. The Judge called the jury into the courthouse even though Elmer was stranded on the freeway:

THE COURT: "I understand the jury has reached a verdict."

THE FOREMAN: "Yes they have, Your Honor."

THE COURT: "Will you hand it to the bailiff? The record will reflect the presence of counsel and the jury panel and the alternate [juror]."

The Court Clerk read the following verdict:

"We, the jury, find for the plaintiff, Elmer Norman, and assess damages as follow:

Compensatory damages, $70,000.

Punitive damages, $4,500,000."

About this time, Elmer arrived at the courthouse. He remembers it this way:

"I came into the courthouse and everybody was still there. The outstanding thing in my mind is how Mr. Shernoff turned around and spied me and he took my hand and shook it and he smiled. Then I heard him say I won and the verdict was $4,500,000. I was stunned. I went out into the hallway and there was all this buzzing and talking. I started to thank the jurors for giving the case such attention, and then the amazing thing was that they thanked me for bringing it to their attention."

Perhaps more than any other case, this verdict demonstrated that no matter how small or infirm a person is, our system of justice allows anyone to make a difference—if he or she is right, and if he or she is persistent. Thanks to Elmer Norman, insurance companies should now think long and hard about taking advantage of older policyholders.

The newspapers made the verdict sound crazy. They just told a story about a senior citizen with a $48 claim who won $4½ million. Without a full explanation of what happened in court, it did sound strange. But the verdict was logical, right, and based upon the evidence. I knew the insurance industry would charge that large punitive awards like this are substantial windfalls like a lottery. In one sense they are. But they are not nearly the windfalls that the insurance industry reaps when it dupes policyholders out of their rightful benefits or delays legitimate payment. Furthermore, whatever windfalls these awards represent, they also have an undeniably therapeutic effect on making the insurance industry more honest as a whole.

Consumer resources

The organizations that follow are excellent resources for anyone interested in heathcare reform, particularly in the battle against managed care companies. Their web sites include, for example, useful information about pending legislation, HMO rankings and legal support, as well as advice on how to file a complaint against your managed care plan. Other resources include your state medical board to check on your doctor's record, your state Department of Insurance, Department of Corporations, and Department of Health to review your HMO's background.

- ASSOCIATION OF TRIAL LAWYERS OF AMERICA
  1050 31st St. NW
  Washington, DC 20007
  ph. 800-424-2725
  web site: http://www.atlanet.org

- CENTER FOR HEALTH DISPUTE RESOLUTION (CHDR)
  1 Fishers Rd., 2nd Fl.
  Pittsford, NY 14534-9597
  ph. 716-586-1770

- CENTER FOR PATIENT ADVOCACY
  1350 Beverly Rd., Ste. 108
  McLean, VA 22101
  ph. 800-846-7444 or 703-748-0400
  web site: http://www.patientadvocacy.org

- CITIZENS FOR CHOICE IN HEALTH CARE
  1954 University Ave. West, Ste. 8
  St. Paul, MN 55104
  ph. 612-646-8935
  web site: http://www.cchc-mn.org

- CONSUMER COALITION FOR QUALITY HEALTH CARE
  1275 K St. NW, Ste. 602
  Washington, DC 20005
  ph. 202-789-3606
  web site: http://www.consumers.org

- CONSUMERS FOR QUALITY CARE
  Jamie Court–Director
  1750 Ocean Park Ave., Ste. 200
  Santa Monica, CA 90405
  ph. 310-392-0522
  web site: http://www.consumerwatchdog.org

- EMPOWER! THE MANAGED CARE PATIENT ADVOCATE
  Co-Med Publications, Inc.
  210 West Washington Square
  Philadelphia, PA 19106
  ph. 215-592-1363
  web site: http://www.comed.com/empower

- FAMILIES USA
  1334 G St. NW, 3rd Fl.
  Washington, DC 20005
  ph. 202-628-3030
  web site: http://www.familiesusa.org

- THE HEALTH ADMINISTRATION RESPONSIBILITY
  PROJECT
  552 12th St.
  Santa Monica, CA 90402
  web site: http://www.harp.org

- JOINT COMMISSION ON ACCREDITATION OF
  HEALTHCARE ORGANIZATIONS
  One Renaissance Blvd.

Oakbrook Terrace, IL 60181
ph. 630-792-5800
web site: http://www.jcaho.org

- NATIONAL ASSOCIATION OF INSURANCE
  COMMISSIONERS (NAIC)
  Consumer Information Center
  Department 59
  Pueblo, CO 81009

- NATIONAL CENTER FOR QUALITY ASSURANCE
  2000 L St., NW, Ste. 500
  Washington, DC 20036
  ph. 202-955-3500
  web site: http://www.ncqa.org

- PACIFIC BUSINESS GROUP ON HEALTH
  33 New Montgomery St., Ste. 1450
  San Francisco, CA 94105
  ph. 888-244-2124 or 415-281-8660
  web site: http://www.healthscope.org

- PHYSICIANS WHO CARE
  10715 Gulfdale, Ste. 275
  San Antonio, TX 78216
  web site: http://www.hmopage.org

- PUBLIC CITIZEN
  Ralph Nader-Founder
  1600 20th St. NW

Washington, DC 20009
web site: http://www.citizen.org

- US DEPARTMENT OF LABOR
Pension and Welfare Benefits Administration
Advice and Complaints About ERISA Plans
200 Constitution Ave. NW
Washington, DC 20210
ph. 202-219-8776
web site: http://www.dol.gov

Are you worried that HMOs and other for-profit health care corporations will put their profits above your health when you are sick?

Consumers For Quality Care (CQC) is working to protect you, your family, and your physician from corporate cost-cutting at HMOs.

In 1994, CQC was established to investigate and report publicly on the epidemic of medical negligence. With the rise of mismanaged care, CQC has become the HMO patient's watchdog:

- exposing abuses at HMOs and championing greater accountability;
- sponsoring federal and state legislation to expand patients' rights and remedies;
- promoting and protecting high quality health care.

Presently, CQC is supporting federal and state-based efforts to end an unintended loophole in the Employees Retirement Income and Security Act or ERISA.

Consumers for Quality ✚ Care

1750 Ocean Park Blvd. #200
Santa Monica, CA 90405
Phone: 310-392-0522
Website: http://www.consumerwatchdog.org

YES, I want to stay informed about efforts to reform the ERISA loophole, and protect working Americans from unsafe HMO medical decisions.

Please keep me updated on this important issue.

NAME _____

ADDRESS _____

CITY _____ STATE _____ ZIP _____

Glossary of Terms

Arbitration—A hearing between two or more parties that is decided by a third party as a means of settling a dispute. Oftentimes, HMOs invoke "arbitration clauses" when their members try to take them to court.

Bad Faith—The unreasonable denial of a legitimate claim. If a policyholder's claim has been unreasonably denied, he/she may be able to collect damages for pain and suffering, consequential damages, punitive damages, etc.

Capitation—A fixed amount of money per patient per year that medical providers receive to provide for all of their patients' medical needs.

Case Management—A system in which an administrator is responsible for determining a patient's access to health and social services.

Claims/Insurance Adjuster—The person responsible for investigating, evaluating, and negotiating a policyholder's claim. Not to be mistaken with the insurance agent who sold the policy.

Cost-Sharing—Provision in a health insurance plan that requires the insured to pay a portion of his or her medical expenses, including co-payments, deductibles, etc.

Custodial Care vs. Skilled Care—Custodial care, such as the care received in a nursing home, is considered custodial. Skilled care is medical in nature, such as intensive care support, life support equipment, etc.

Deductible—A fixed amount of money the patient is required to pay before the insurance coverage kicks in.

Disability—An illness or injury that leaves the insured unable to perform work-related tasks.

Drug Formulary—A list of approved prescription medications for use by the health plan which are dispensed through participating pharmacies to the member participant.

Exclusions—Services or procedures that the insurer excludes from coverage because they are deemed "experimental" or because the patient's condition is labeled pre-existing, etc.

Fee-For-Service—Traditional health care coverage where the patient or insurance company is billed for each test or service performed.

Gag Clause/Gag Rule—A provision in some managed care contracts that forbids doctors from discussing all available treatment options/financial incentives with patients.

Gatekeeper—A primary care doctor in an HMO who coordinates all diagnostic testing and specialty referrals required for a patient's medical care.

Health Maintenance Organization (HMO)—A type of health plan that provides services to members for a set fee through an open or closed network of providers.

Managed Care—A system in which all medical treatment and payments are approved or denied by the insurer.

Medicare—Government health insurance program for the elderly and disabled.

Open Access—HMOs which allow members to self-refer for specialty care without a referral from a primary care physician.

Open Enrollment—A period of time when individuals may enroll or change their health benefits program.

Point-of-Service—A health plan that allows the patient to select the method of payment (traditional, PPO or HMO) at the time service is received.

Portability—An insurance provision that allows individuals to keep their insurance when they change jobs.

Pre-Certification—The process of getting treatment pre-approved.

Pre-Existing Condition—An illness or condition that an individual has before he/she obtains an insurance policy. Many insurers refuse to issue policies or pay for care for pre-existing conditions or may not pay for that condition for a set period of time.

Premium—The amount of money paid for the insurance benefits to be provided by a policy.

Primary Care—Basic or general care as opposed to specialized care.

Punitive Damages—Monetary award to deter or punish a company for its fraudulent behavior.

Reasonable and Customary—Charges that an insurer will pay for a given procedure. Insurers may use outdated fee schedules or fee data from geographical areas that are not comparable to where a policyholder was treated.

Rescission—The act of denying a claim or even canceling an insurance policy due to nondisclosure of a patient's medical history, pre-existing condition, etc.

Third-Party Claims—Claims made against another person's insurance company. *Example:* You sue a condominium owner's insurer when you sustain injuries due to the balcony giving way.

Underwriting—The act of investigating a claim.

About the Firm...

SHERNOFF, BIDART, DARRAS & ARKIN is a nationally recognized leader of insurance bad faith law on behalf of individual and business consumers. The firm specializes in representing policyholders in all types of insurance law, including medical, HMO, life, disability, homeowners, property, and all types of liability insurance, and it has established an international reputation as a leader in Holocaust-era life insurance litigation.

William M. Shernoff, the firm's senior partner, has more than 25 years of experience representing consumers. He is the father of bad faith law in California, having persuaded the California Supreme Court in 1979 to establish new case law that permits plaintiffs to sue insurance companies for bad faith when they intentionally take advantage of policyholders. Mr. Shernoff co-authored the legal textbook *Insurance Bad Faith Litigation*, which has become the field's definitive treatise, as well as *How To Make Insurance Companies Pay Your Claims…And What To Do If They Don't* and *Payment Refused*. Mr. Shernoff has been featured in the *New York Times, Wall Street Journal,* and *Time Magazine*, as well as appearing on "60 Minutes." He is a past President of Consumer Attorneys Association of California and has been voted "Trial Lawyer of the Year" by Consumer Attorneys Association of Los Angeles.

Michael J. Bidart is the firm's expert on property, homeowners, casualty, and commercial insurance bad faith litigation. An active political advocate and a frequent lecturer on bad faith insurance practices, Mr. Bidart was the counsel of record in a landmark decision known as *Allegro v. State Farm* (1996), which established groundbreaking new case law for suing insurance companies doing business in California.

Frank N. Darras is a nationally recognized expert in health and disability litigation, including catastrophic injury cases. A frequent lecturer on disability issues and bad faith practices, Mr. Darras authored the chapters in this book entitled "Traps in Company-Provided Disability Insurance" and "The Right Disability Coverage."

Sharon J. Arkin is the firm's expert on appellate law and legal writing. She has authored numerous articles and seminar materials, including "Plaintiff Strategies to Make the Most of Managed Care Claims" and "The Tragedies of ERISA: How the Supreme Court Turned ERISA on Its Head." Ms. Arkin frequently testifies before California legislative and regulatory committees on behalf of consumers.

Timothy P. Dillon specializes in life insurance cases and class-actions. He has been responsible for refunding millions of dollars to life insurance policyholders through his life insurance class action suits.

Shernoff, Bidart, Darras & Arkin is located at 600 S. Indian Hill Boulevard, Claremont, CA 91711-5498, Tel. 909-621-4935 or 800-458-3351, Fax: 909-625-6915.

HOW TO CONTACT US

Please take a moment to fill out the questionnaire below if you would like to obtain more information about health care reform, if you are experiencing difficulties with your HMO and need legal advice, or if you have another insurance-related question.

☐ **YES!** I would like to talk with someone regarding a health care problem or other insurance-related matter. (*Note:* There is no fee for a consultation appointment. If you check this box, somebody will contact you.)

☐ **YES!** I am very interested in health care reform and I would like to learn more about how I can get involved.

Comments:_____

_____

_____

_____

SHERNOFF, BIDART, DARRAS & ARKIN
600 South Indian Hill Boulevard
Claremont, CA 91711
909-621-4935
800-458-3351
Fax: 909-625-6915